D1417097

NEWMAN AND GLADSTONE:

The Vatican Decrees

With an Introduction by

A L V A N   S.   R Y A N

UNIVERSITY OF NOTRE DAME PRESS · 1962

Copyright 1962 by

UNIVERSITY OF NOTRE DAME PRESS
NOTRE DAME, INDIANA

First Paperback Edition

"The Vatican Decrees in their Bearing on Civil Allegiance: A Political Expostulation," by Rt. Hon. W. E. Gladstone, M.P., was first published in 1874 in London by John Murray, Albemarle Street. "A Letter Addressed to His Grace the Duke of Norfolk on Occasion of Mr. Gladstone's Recent Expostulation," by John Henry Newman, D.D., was first published in 1875 in London by B. M. Pickering, 196 Piccadilly.

Manufactured in the United States of America

NEWMAN AND GLADSTONE:
The Vatican Decrees

INTRODUCTION

This reprinting of Gladstone's "Vatican Decrees in Their Bearing on Civil Allegiance: A Political Expostulation" (1874) and Newman's reply in his "Letter to the Duke of Norfolk" (1875) makes the two works available once again not only to the scholar but to a wider reading public. The controversy has both an historical interest and the most urgent contemporary relevance. From the moment when Christ, questioned as to the image of Caesar on the coin handed Him by the Pharisees, replied, "Render, therefore, to Caesar the things that are Caesar's, and to God the things that are God's," the relation of Church and State has been a classical problem of Christendom. If the general principle is immutable, the application in a given historical situation is complex and difficult, as the sharp disagreements even among those with a common faith make abundantly evident. Perhaps the most to be hoped for is that wherever the opportunity still exists the centuries-old debate can continue in a calm and reasonable atmosphere.

For me even to attempt any systematic adjudication of the issues between Gladstone and Newman would be an impertinence. My purpose in this introduction is more modest. It is, first, to suggest the personal associations and the contemporary issues in England and on the Continent out of which the debate arose; secondly, to comment briefly on what I take to be the most significant aspects of the controversy; and finally, to call attention to parallel examples in America.

II

The Gladstone-Newman controversy is in one sense, at least, like an iceberg; there is massive conflict beneath the surface far larger than the one immediately visible. Both Gladstone and Newman had already taken part in this dialogue for some forty years when their essays appeared. Tracing its outlines can serve to clarify their interpretations, the kind of evidence they present, the tone they adopt, the allusions they employ.

The religious convictions of William E. Gladstone (1809-1898) were a curious blend of high Anglicanism and the Evangelical piety imbued in him by his mother. Even though he left Oxford just before the start of the Oxford Movement, he was close to such men as Hope-Scott and Manning. In 1838 he had published a book entitled *The State in Its Relations with the Church* in which he defended a virtually theocratic absorption of the State by the Church. Yet in one of the most crucial issues of the 1850's, the Gorham Case, he strongly objected to state interference with the spiritual prerogatives of the Anglican Church. (It was this case, incidentally, that was indirectly responsible for Manning's conversion to the Roman Catholic Church.) Gladstone's stand on these issues is significant because, in the light of his later attitudes, it shows an ambiguity in his thinking on Church and State. If we can discount his first book as expressing a theory he soon abandoned, we can say that he took the Anglican Church as representing the norm in the relation of Church and State. Yet it has to be emphasized that Gladstone had an honorable record as a defender of Catholic liberties, and also that the disestablishment of the Irish Church was an act of his last administration.

Gladstone's admiration for Newman was deep. He called his conversion a calamity for the Anglican Church. And in his "Expostulation" he speaks of Newman as the foremost living theologian in the Catholic Church. But the Catholic he was closest to was John Acton. After Acton's early years of study at Munich under von Döllinger, from whom he learned the methods of historical investigation and caught the passion for liberty that guided his entire subsequent career, he entered the House of Commons as a Liberal member in 1859. His acquaintance with Gladstone, 25 years his senior, soon developed into a close friendship. Here, then, were two members of the Liberal Party, one Anglican, the other Roman Catholic, working together in the political sphere and both vitally concerned with the civil and religious issues of the period.

Through Acton, Gladstone followed closely the criticisms directed by von Döllinger at the policies of the Papacy. Acton, for example, was influential from 1857-1864 in shaping the editorial policies of two liberal Catholic periodicals, *The Rambler* and its successor, *The Home and Foreign Review*. The articles which Döllinger contributed were severely criticized, as was Acton's own article on the Munich Conference of 1864, which he had attended with von Döllinger. The *Review* would have been censured had not Acton terminated it with the April, 1864, issue.

Gladstone and Acton were in Rome together in 1866, and it was while Acton was in Rome for the Vatican Council in 1869 that Gladstone recommended his elevation to the peerage. This bare outline of the relations among the then Prime Minister, Lord Acton, and von Döllinger brings us to the Vatican Council.

While the Vatican Council first assembled on December 8, 1869, the question of defining the dogma of infallibility had already been discussed for many months, and von Döllinger had taken an active part. The sharp division of opinion between those like Manning and W. G. Ward who favored the definition, and the inopportunists, of whom Newman, at least for a time, was one, though he was not present at the Council, is well known. Acton's role, a real cloak-and-dagger episode by some accounts, was certainly an active one. He did all he could to prevent the definition. He urged the British Government to interfere; he wrote back accounts of the proceedings to Gladstone, the Prime Minister; and he kept Döllinger informed through letters in which the names of participants were in cypher. These, combined with other letters, were published in the *Augsburger Allgemeine Zeitung* starting in December, 1869, under the name Quirinus, and later in English as *Letters from Rome on the Council* (1870).

When the dogma of Papal Infallibility was adopted by the Council in July of 1870, Acton was already at his home in Bavaria, where he immediately wrote and published a monograph based on the anti-infallibilist views at the Council. His friend Döllinger refused to accept the definition and on April 1, 1871, was excommunicated. He did not, however, join the Old Catholic movement formed in Munich in September of that year.

What is significant here is Gladstone's close interest in the views of the party within the Catholic Church that opposed the definition. There is evident in his essay not only his personal interpretation, as an Anglican and a statesman, of the relation of Church and State, but in addition, a juxtaposing, out of intimate knowledge, of the two extreme wings of the Council against one another, and the identification of the Papacy itself, present and future, with the most intransigent group.

In a sense, Newman recapitulates in his reply to Gladstone many of the views of a lifetime, as the briefest review of his earlier attitudes will make clear. As a leader of the Oxford Movement from 1833 until his conversion in 1845, he had opposed Erastianism, the subordination of the Church to the State. The crisis came with Tract 90, in which Newman held that the Thirty-nine Articles would bear a Catholic interpretation. To Newman in these years the chief danger to the Anglican Church was religious liberalism. While he was no less a foe of religious liberalism after his conversion, he found among many of his fellow Catholics an unimaginative and authoritarian conservatism which led him into a series of disputes and difficulties in the 50's and 60's.

From 1857 to 1864 Newman was connected, for example, with *The Rambler* and *The Home and Foreign Review* in an advisory capacity, and briefly as editor of *The Rambler*. It was his interest in these reviews that first brought him into association with Acton. The position these two reviews took on philosophical, social, and political issues — and their sometimes reckless incursions into the area of theology — did not always satisfy Newman, by any means, yet he saw the need for a bold facing of difficult questions. Opposing as he did the conservatism of *The Dublin Review,* then under W. G. Ward's editorship, and trying without success to moderate the tone of the liberal reviews, Newman finally refused to write for either.

The publication in December, 1864, of the encyclical of Pope Pius IX, *Quanta Cura,* together with the *Syllabus of Errors,* immediately aroused a storm of controversy. The Ultramontane group in the Church applauded the appearance of the two documents without reservation, and made few distinctions between them. W. G. Ward, for example, wrote to the *Weekly Register* stating that the encyclical and the *Syllabus* were unquestionably the Church's infallible utterances. Newman, on the contrary, sided with such moderates as Bishop Dupanloup against English Catholics like Manning and W. G. Ward and the Continental school best represented by Louis Veuillot, editor of the French publication *Univers.* One letter of Newman's to Ambrose St. John, directly after the encyclical and *Syllabus* were published, is indicative. He writes: "It is

difficult to know *what he* [the Pope] *means* by his condemnation. The words 'myth,' 'non-interference,' 'progress,' 'toleration,' are undefined. . . . For the rest, all I can say (*entre
nous*) is that the advisers of the Holy Father seem determined
to make our position in England as difficult as ever they can."
(Wilfrid Ward, *Life of John Henry Cardinal Newman* [Lon-
don, 1912; 2 vols.], II, 80.)

The moderation and the concern for precision evident in
Newman's attitude on numerous similar issues during this
period brought on him the charge of "minimizing" the claims
of the Catholic Church from those who were convinced that
"maximizing" was the need of the age, and he refers to the
charge more than once in his reply to Gladstone.

III

While the publication of *Quanta Cura* and the *Syllabus* and
later the defining of Papal Infallibility, are the ostensible
subjects of Gladstone's "Expostulation," certain more personal
events, which he touches on, are important. I refer especially
to the failure of his Irish University Bill, owing largely to the
opposition of the Irish Bishop, his retirement from the leader-
ship of the Liberal Party at the end of his First Ministry in
1874, and his renewal of his friendship with von Döllinger,
whose excommunication he saw as the result of the aggressive
policies of Rome. Finally, he took Manning's recently published lecture on "Caesarism and Ultramontanism," which
indicated no such limitations on Papal supremacy as Newman was to make, as an expression official Roman policy.

Gladstone put forth his objections first in an essay in the *Contemporary Review,* and then wrote his "Expostulation" to develop his charges in more detail.

The proportions of Gladstone's "Expostulation" are significant. His first and fourth propositions on the Church's alleged break with tradition and repudiation of modern thought are treated together, and very briefly. There is, to say the least, a certain irony in Gladstone's attempt to enlist Newman, for whom the writing of *The Development of Christian Doctrine* in 1845 had been a demonstration of the continuity of modern Catholicism with the ancient church, in support of the charge of "new doctrine." To his second proposition on the refurbishing of "rusty tools," Gladstone devotes somewhat more space. The point of attack here is the *Syllabus of Errors.* Gladstone selects all but the first and fourth of his eighteen condemned propositions from the eighty listed as condemned in the *Syllabus.* It should be noted that he does not give them as listed in the *Syllabus,* but in abbreviated form, and he gives none of the references to the contexts of earlier encyclicals and allocutions where these propositions were originally treated. Most important, he holds that the author of the propositions (according to him the Pope, though Newman says in his "Letter" that "there is not a word in it of the Pope's own writing") claims "a sole and unlimited power to interpret them in such manner and by such rules as he may from time to time think fit." Moreover, in linking the encyclical *Quanta Cura* and the *Syllabus* without distinction, Gladstone indentifies the extremist views of W. G. Ward, Veuillot, and others, with the official Catholic interpretation. Aside from certain inaccuracies in his manner of condensing propositions already extremely brief, pointed out by Newman (and even more fully by Canon Neville), Gladstone makes a strong case against what must be recognized as a then widely-held view of the *Syllabus*. It was a view Newman had repudiated from 1864 on, and hence Newman devotes some of the most closely-reasoned pages in his "Letter" to the interpretation of the *Syllabus*.

The nub of Gladstone's "Expostulation" is his third proposition. To it he devotes nearly half of the entire essay. Beginning by praising Döllinger for his opposition to the Definition of Infallibility, he asks if converts to the Catholic Church forfeit mental and moral freedom, and answers with historical references. In the process he makes the statement that the Popes had kept up "for well-nigh a thousand years their claim to dogmatic infallibility." This undercuts, of course, his first proposition that the "decrees" repudiated tradition and introduced something new. (In "Vaticanism," published after Newman's "Letter," Gladstone retracted the statement as a "slip of the pen" made with "culpable inadvertence.") The historical references emphasize the statements of Catholics just prior to the Catholic Emancipation Act of 1829. Compared with Newman's way of putting things, such statements as Bishop Doyle's certainly lack precision, as Newman's "Letter" admits. The earlier assurances, reasons Gladstone, have been abrogated by the encyclical of 1864, the *Syllabus,* and the Vatican Council. Since "an absolute and entire Obedience" in faith and morals and "all things which concern the discipline and government of the Church" is demanded of Catholics, and since moral issues enter into virtually every phase of life — so Gladstone reasons — "it is the supreme direction of us in respect to all Duty, which the Pontiff declares to belong to him. . . ." Hence he concludes that "the loyalty and civil duty" of Catholics are at the mercy of the Pope.

Newman's "Letter" is more than a plea for precision, for distinctions and discriminations, though it is certainly that. It is a continuing demonstration of his ability to make such distinctions and to disentangle the relevant from the irrelevant. While his tone is frequently crisp and ironic, it is also frequently sympathetic. However sharply he attempts to refute Gladstone's charges, he treats him with respect, and alludes with sadness to the alienation of "so religious a mind." It is clear throughout the essay that Newman is as much concerned to distinguish his views of Church and State from those of many influential fellow Catholics as to answer Gladstone's charges. In the breadth of its purpose, the "Letter" is like the *Apologia,* and in many ways is an indispensable supplement to it.

Newman announces in his Introductory Remarks that he will confine himself chiefly to Gladstone's charge against the loyalty of Catholics, and this receives major attention. But Gladstone's other charges are also answered. In fact a comparison of the two pamphlets suggests that Newman's ten sections can be read somewhat as follows: leaving aside introduction and conclusion, the second and third sections answer Gladstone's first and fourth propositions, the fourth and fifth sections answer the third proposition, the sixth and seventh sections answer the second proposition, and the eighth and ninth sections, while concerned with the Vatican Council and the Vatican Definition, also bear directly or indirectly on Gladstone's third proposition.

To Gladstone's charge of "new doctrine" and the repudiation of ancient history, Newman answers by comparing the Ancient Church and the Papal Church, stressing the fact that it was the continuity between the two that led so many into the Roman Catholic Church at the time of the Oxford Movement. Here I think the effectiveness of Newman's reply can be questioned, since Gladstone's charge was chiefly aimed at events and situations subsequent to 1845. The next sections, on "Divided Allegiance" and "Conscience," are the heart of Newman's reply. In the first of these he defines carefully the nature of obedience and authority as he understands them, making a comparison between the jurisdiction which the civil law exercises over Englishmen and the authority of the Pope over members of the Church. If the former circumscribes our liberties in various ways, "the thraldom and irksomeness is nothing compared with the great blessings which the Constitution and legislature secure to us." So it is with the relation of the Catholic to the Church. Newman analyzes Gladstone's phrase "supreme direction," emphasizes the role of moral theology in the direction of Catholics, and affirms that the weight of the Pope's "hand upon us, as private men, is absolutely unappreciable." Yet he concludes this section by citing hypothetical cases in which the jurisdictions of Church and State might come into conflict. In some he would obey the Queen; in others, he would obey the Pope.

Newman's section on "Conscience" is perhaps even more

important. To Gladstone's statement that the Catholic owes absolute and entire obedience to the Pope, Newman answers with further distinctions. The Pope is the Vicar of Christ on earth and the visible head of the Church, but "Conscience is the aboriginal Vicar of Christ. . . ." It is "the voice of God in the nature and heart of man, as distinct from the voice of Revelation." It is a strong position that Newman takes here, and he gives it a dramatic memorableness with his famous comment that if he were to drink a toast to the Pope, he would drink to conscience first, and to the Pope afterwards.

The care with which Newman defines what he means by conscience suggests his recognition of how easily he might be misinterpreted. He quotes St. Thomas Aquinas and St. Augustine, making clear that what he means by conscience is the recognition of the Natural Law. Moreover, he is careful to contrast the true idea of conscience as held by Protestants and Catholics alike, and the false notion of conscience prevalent in "the world of philosophy" and in the popular mind. His distinction hinges essentially on the contrast between the acknowledgment of a Moral Governor and the definition of conscience as a merely human norm. Thus he explains how it is that Pope Pius speaks against "liberty of conscience." It is the second, the false, meaning of conscience he and other Popes have attacked, whereas "did the Pope speak against Conscience in the true sense of the word, he would commit a suicidal act."

These two sections of Newman's "Letter" have notable parallels. In both, one has the impression that Newman considers his subject extremely complex, and in need of the most precise discriminations if misunderstanding is to be avoided. In both, he ends with hypothetical cases of "divided allegiance" in which his decisions are clearly presented. Finally, in both, he sees the necessity for sharp distinctions: in "Divided Allegiance" he speaks of following his own judgment in rare cases; whereas Private Judgment is the normal rule for Protestants. In "Conscience" he discriminates his view of conscience from others widely held.

IV

The Gladstone-Newman exchange is clearly but part of a controversy over the claims of Church and State that echoed throughout Europe and Great Britain in the third quarter of the 19th century. And there was a parallel conflict in America in which Orestes Brownson took a position similar to Newman's in many ways, though surprisingly different in others.

In the "Native Americanism" issue and the Know-Nothing Movement of the 1850's, the central question was the relation of Catholicity to the American political and social tradition. Brownson's essays on these subjects, in which he distinguished sharply between the Catholic Church and the European cultures with which historically it had been associated, aroused the opposition of many American Catholics, especially those of Irish origin. It was in fact because of the repercussions in Ireland that Newman withdrew in 1854 the invitation made to Brownson in 1853 to join the faculty of the new Catholic University in Dublin. In the late 1850's and the early 1860's

Brownson's sympathies were increasingly with the Catholic liberals of Europe. His essays on "Lacordaire and Catholic Progress" (1862), on "Civil and Religious Freedom" (1864), and many of his other essays of this period can be profitably read in the context of the issues debated by Gladstone and Newman.

An even closer counterpart to Newman's "Letter" can be found in certain sections of Brownson's *The American Republic* (1866). Like Newman, Brownson develops the distinction between the domains of Church and State. Like Newman he sees the importance of a pluralistic approach, and like Newman he rejects either a theocratic absorption of State in Church or a totalitarian elevation of the State into a false Church claiming dominion over both the civil and the spiritual.

Where Brownson and Newman come to very different conclusions is on the interpretation of the *Syllabus of Errors*. Brownson's essays on Church and State issues just prior to the publication of the *Syllabus* were the object of continuous and sharp attack from ultra-conservatives in the Church. Their criticism, plus more personal reasons, led him to suspend *Brownson's Quarterly Review* with the issue of October, 1864. When the *Syllabus* appeared in December, his critics immediately interpreted it as a condemnation of many of his recent writings. Surprisingly, in view of Brownson's acumen and his capacity for logical analysis, he came to the same conclusion. He made none of the distinctions as to what was, and was not, condemned that Newman did, and the whole tenor of his revived *Review* in the three years from 1873 to

1875, the very year Newman's "Letter" appeared, is extremely conservative.

Finally, the controversy has so many implications for the present that one can only suggest them, and raise a few questions. It is a paradox that the renouncing of "mental and moral freedom" Gladstone alluded to has been demanded in whole areas of the earth by regimes that are as much opposed to those liberal principles Gladstone wishes to defend as they are to the Catholic Church. Perhaps there were implications in Gladstone's view of the claims of civil society which he did not see, and which he would have drawn back from in dismay if he had seen them. But, on the other hand, and again in the light of recent history, perhaps he was rightly alarmed at some of the extravagant claims of many Catholic spokesmen, however wrongly he identified their views with those of the Universal Church.

Harold J. Laski, in *Studies in the Problems of Sovereignty* (New Haven 1917), has called Newman's "Letter," along with work by Sir Henry Maine and F. W. Maitland, "the profoundest discussion of the nature of obedience and of sovereignty to be found in the English language. . ." (p. 202). Whether or not one fully agrees, Newman's "Letter" is certainly one of the most important discussions of the issue. Today there is a renewed interest not only in the problem Newman deals with, but also in the very approach he makes to its resolution. I refer especially to his emphasis on the natural law and conscience, and to the care with which he defined the respective jurisdictions of Church and State. For example, comparing John Courtney Murray's recently

published *We Hold These Truths* with Newman's "Letter,"
one notes both striking similarities and significant differences
of emphasis. The reprinting of the Gladstone-Newman debate
should encourage the dialogue that Murray's book has spoken
of as essential to a valid civil consensus.

Alvan S. Ryan

Saarbrücken, Germany
November, 1961

NEWMAN AND GLADSTONE:
The Vatican Decrees

THE VATICAN DECREES

IN THEIR BEARING ON

CIVIL ALLEGIANCE:

A POLITICAL EXPOSTULATION.

BY THE

RIGHT HON. W. E. GLADSTONE, M.P.

LONDON:

JOHN MURRAY, ALBEMARLE STREET.

1874.

LONDON:
PRINTED BY WILLIAM CLOWES AND SONS,
STAMFORD STREET AND CHARING CROSS.

CONTENTS.

———

THE VATICAN DECREES

IN THEIR BEARING ON

CIVIL ALLEGIANCE.

I. THE OCCASION AND SCOPE OF THIS TRACT.

IN the prosecution of a purpose not polemical but
pacific, I have been led to employ words which belong,
more or less, to the region of religious controversy;
and which, though they were themselves few, seem to
require, from the various feelings they have aroused,
that I should carefully define, elucidate, and defend
them. The task is not of a kind agreeable to me;
but I proceed to perform it.

Among the causes, which have tended to disturb
and perplex the public mind in the consideration of
our own religious difficulties, one has been a certain
alarm at the aggressive activity and imagined growth
of the Roman Church in this country. All are aware
of our susceptibility on this side; and it was not, I
think, improper for one who desires to remove everything that can interfere with a calm and judicial
temper, and who believes the alarm to be groundless

to state, pointedly though briefly, some reasons for that belief.

Accordingly I did not scruple to use the following language, in a paper inserted in the number of the 'Contemporary Review' for the month of October. I was speaking of "the question whether a handful of the clergy are or are not engaged in an utterly hopeless and visionary effort to Romanise the Church and people of England."

" At no time since the bloody reign of Mary has such a scheme been possible. But if it had been possible in the seventeenth or eighteenth centuries, it would still have become impossible in the nineteenth : when Rome has substituted for the proud boast of *semper eadem* a policy of violence and change in faith ; when she has refurbished, and paraded anew, every rusty tool she was fondly thought to have disused ; when no one can become her convert without renouncing his moral and mental freedom, and placing his civil loyalty and duty at the mercy of another ; and when she has equally repudiated modern thought and ancient history."*

Had I been, when I wrote this passage, as I now am, addressing myself in considerable measure to my Roman Catholic fellow-countrymen, I should have striven to avoid the seeming roughness of some of these expressions; but as the question is now about

---

* 'Contemporary Review,' Oct. 1874, p. 674.

their substance, from which I am not in any particular disposed to recede, any attempt to recast their general form would probably mislead. I proceed, then, to deal with them on their merits.

More than one friend of mine, among those who have been led to join the Roman Catholic communion, has made this passage the subject, more or less, of expostulation. Now, in my opinion, the assertions which it makes are, as coming from a layman who has spent most and the best years of his life in the observation and practice of politics, not aggressive but defensive.

It is neither the abettors of the Papal Chair, nor any one who, however far from being an abettor of the Papal Chair, actually writes from a Papal point of view, that has a right to remonstrate with the world at large; but it is the world at large, on the contrary, that has the fullest right to remonstrate, first with His Holiness, secondly with those who share his proceedings, thirdly even with such as passively allow and accept them.

I therefore, as one of the world at large, propose to expostulate in my turn. I shall strive to show to such of my Roman Catholic fellow-subjects as may kindly give me a hearing that, after the singular steps which the authorities of their Church have in these last years thought fit to take, the people of this country, who fully believe in their loyalty, are entitled, on purely civil grounds, to expect from them some declaration or manifestation of opinion, in reply to that ecclesiastical party in their Church who have laid down, in their name, principles adverse to the purity and integrity of civil allegiance.

Undoubtedly my allegations are of great breadth. Such broad allegations require a broad and a deep foundation. The first question which they raise is, Are they, as to the material part of them, true? But even their truth might not suffice to show that their publication was opportune. The second question, then, which they raise is, Are they, for any practical purpose, material? And there is yet a third, though a minor, question, which arises out of the propositions in connection with their authorship, Were they suitable to be set forth by the present writer?

To these three questions I will now set myself to reply. And the matter of my reply will, as I conceive, constitute and convey an appeal to the understandings of my Roman Catholic fellow-countrymen, which I trust that, at the least, some among them may deem not altogether unworthy of their consideration.

From the language used by some of the organs of Roman Catholic opinion, it is, I am afraid, plain that in some quarters they have given deep offence. Displeasure, indignation, even fury, might be said to mark the language which in the heat of the moment has been expressed here and there. They have been hastily treated as an attack made upon Roman Catholics generally, nay, as an insult offered them. It is obvious to reply, that of Roman Catholics generally they state nothing. Together with a reference to " converts," of which I shall say more, they constitute generally a free and strong animadversion on the conduct of the Papal Chair, and of its advisers and abettors. If I am told that he who animadverts upon these assails thereby, or insults, Roman Catholics at large, who do not choose their ecclesiastical rulers, and are not recognised as having any voice in the government of their Church, I cannot be bound by or accept a proposition which seems to me to be so little in accordance with reason.

Before all things, however, I should desire it to be understood that, in the remarks now offered, I desire to eschew not only religious bigotry, but likewise theological controversy. Indeed, with theology, except in its civil bearing, with theology as such, I have here nothing whatever to do. But it is the peculiarity of Roman theology that, by thrusting itself into the temporal domain, it naturally, and even necessarily, comes to be a frequent theme of political discussion. To quiet-minded Roman Catholics, it must be a subject of infinite annoyance, that their religion is, on this ground more than any other, the subject of criticism ; more than any other, the occasion of conflicts with the State and of civil disquietude. I feel sincerely how much hardship their case entails. But this hardship is brought upon them altogether by the conduct of the authorities of their own Church.

Why did theology enter so largely into the debates of Parliament on Roman Catholic Emancipation? Certainly not because our statesmen and debaters of fifty years ago had an abstract love of such controversies, but because it was extensively believed that the Pope of Rome had been and was a trespasser upon ground which belonged to the civil authority, and that he affected to determine by spiritual prerogative questions of the civil sphere. This fact, if fact it be, and not the truth or falsehood, the reasonableness or unreasonableness, of any article of purely religious belief, is the whole and sole cause of the mischief. To this fact, and to this fact alone, my language is referable : but for this fact, it would have been neither my duty nor my desire to use it. All other Christian bodies are content with freedom in their own religious domain. Orientals, Lutherans, Calvinists, Presbyterians, Episcopalians, Nonconformists, one and all, in the present day, contentedly and thankfully accept the benefits of civil order; never pretend that the State is not its own master; make no religious claims to temporal possessions or advantages ; and, consequently, never are in perilous collision with the State. Nay more, even so I believe it is with the mass of Roman Catholics individually. But not so with the leaders of their Church, or with those who take pride in following the leaders. Indeed, this has been made matter of boast :—

. " There is not another Church so called" (than the Roman),

" nor any community professing to be a Church, which does not submit, or obey, or hold its peace, when the civil governors of the world command."—' The Present Crisis of the Holy See,' by H. E. Manning, D.D. London, 1861, p. 75.

The Rome of the Middle Ages claimed universal monarchy. The modern Church of Rome has abandoned nothing, retracted nothing. Is that all? Far from it. By condemning (as will be seen) those who, like Bishop Doyle in 1826,* charge the mediæval Popes with aggression, she unconditionally, even if covertly, maintains what the mediæval Popes maintained. But even this is not the worst. The worst by far is that whereas, in the national Churches and communities of the Middle Ages, there was a brisk, vigorous, and constant opposition to these outrageous claims, an opposition which stoutly asserted its own orthodoxy, which always caused itself to be respected, and which even sometimes gained the upper hand; now, in this nineteenth century of ours, and while it is growing old, this same opposition has been put out of court, and judicially extinguished within the Papal Church, by the recent decrees of the Vatican. And it is impossible for persons accepting those decrees justly to complain, when such documents are subjected in good faith to a strict examination as respects their compatibility with civil right and the obedience of subjects.

---

* Lords' Committee, March 18, 1826. Report, p. 190.

In defending my language, I shall carefully mark its limits.   But all defence is reassertion, which properly requires a deliberate reconsideration; and no man who thus reconsiders should scruple, if he find so much as a word that may convey a false impression, to amend it.   Exactness in stating truth according to the measure of our intelligence, is an indispensable condition of justice, and of a title to be heard.

My propositions, then, as they stood, are these : —

1. That " Rome has substituted for the proud boast of *semper eadem*, a policy of violence and change in faith."

2. That she has refurbished and paraded anew every rusty tool she was fondly thought to have disused.

3. That no one can now become her convert without renouncing his moral and mental freedom, and placing his civil loyalty and duty at the mercy of another.

4. That she ("Rome") has equally repudiated modern thought and ancient history.

II. The First and the Fourth Propositions.

Of the first and fourth of these propositions I shall dispose rather summarily, as they appear to belong to the theological domain.   They refer to a fact, and they record an opinion.   One fact to which they refer is this : that, in days within my memory, the constant, favourite, and imposing argument of Roman controversialists was the unbroken and absolute identity in belief of the Roman Church from the days of our Saviour until now. No one, who has at all followed the course of this literature during the last forty years, can fail to be sensible of the change in its present tenour. More and more have the assertions of continuous uniformity of doctrine receded into scarcely penetrable shadow. More and more have another series of assertions, of a living authority, ever ready to open, adopt, and shape Christian doctrine according to the times, taken their place. Without discussing the abstract compatibility of these lines of argument, I note two of the immense practical differences between them. In the first, the office claimed by the Church is principally that of a witness to facts ; in the second, principally that of a judge, if not a revealer, of doctrine. In the first, the processes which the Church undertakes are subject to a constant challenge and appeal to history ; in the second, no amount of historical testimony can avail against the unmeasured power of the theory of development. Most important, most pregnant considerations, these, at least for two classes of persons : for those who think that exaggerated doctrines of Church power are among the real and serious dangers of the age ; and for those who think that against all forms, both of superstition and of unbelief, one main preservative is to be found in maintaining the truth and authority of history, and the inestimable value of the historic spirit.

So much for the fact; as for the opinion, that the recent Papal decrees are at war with modern thought, and that, purporting to enlarge the necessary creed of Christendom, they involve a violent breach with history, this is a matter unfit for me to discuss, as it is a question of Divinity; but not unfit for me to have mentioned in my article; since the opinion given there is the opinion of those with whom I was endeavouring to reason, namely, the great majority of the British public.

If it is thought that the word violence was open to exception, I regret I cannot give it up. The justification of the ancient definitions of the Church, which have endured the storms of 1500 years, was to be found in this, that they were not arbitrary or wilful, but that they wholly sprang from, and related to theories rampant at the time, and regarded as menacing to Christian belief. Even the Canons of the Council of Trent have in the main this amount, apart from their matter, of presumptive warrant. But the decrees of the present perilous Pontificate have been passed to favour and precipitate prevailing currents of opinion in the ecclesiastical world of Rome. The growth of what is often termed among Protestants Mariolatry, and of belief in Papal Infallibility, was notoriously advancing, but it seems not

fast enough to satisfy the dominant party.   To aim
the deadly blows of 1854* and 1870 at the old
historic, scientific, and moderate school, was surely
an act of violence; and with this censure the proceeding of 1870 has actually been visited by the first
living theologian now within the Roman Communion,
I mean, Dr. John Henry Newman; who has used
these significant words, among others : " Why should
an aggressive and insolent faction be allowed to make
the heart of the just sad, whom the Lord hath not
made sorrowful ?" †

III. THE SECOND PROPOSITION.

I take next my second Proposition : that Rome has
refurbished, and paraded anew, every rusty tool she
was fondly thought to have disused.

Is this then a fact, or is it not ?

I must assume that it is denied; and therefore I
cannot wholly pass by the work of proof.   But I will
state in the fewest possible words, and with references, a few propositions, all the holders of which have
been *condemned* by the See of Rome during my own
generation, and especially within the last twelve or
fifteen years.   And, in order that I may do nothing
towards importing passion into what is matter of

---

* Decree of the Immaculate Conception.

† See the remarkable Letter of Dr. Newman to Bishop Ullathorne, in the ' Guardian ' of April 6. 1870.

pure argument, I will avoid citing any of the fear-
fully energetic epithets in which the condemnations
are sometimes clothed.

1. Those who maintain the Liberty of the Press.
Encyclical Letter of Pope Gregory XVI., in 1831 :
and of Pope Pius IX., in 1864.

2. Or the liberty of conscience and of worship.
Encyclical of Pius IX., December 8, 1864.

3. Or the liberty of speech. 'Syllabus' of March 18,
1861. Prop. lxxix. Encyclical of Pope Pius IX.,
December 8, 1864.

4. Or who contend that Papal judgments and
decrees may, without sin, be disobeyed, or differed
from, unless they treat of the rules (*dogmata*) of
faith or morals. Ibid.

5. Or who assign to the State the power of defining
the civil rights (*jura*) and province of the Church.
'Syllabus' of Pope Pius IX., March 8, 1861. Ibid.
Prop. xix.

6. Or who hold that Roman Pontiffs and Ecumenical Councils have transgressed the limits of
their power, and usurped the rights of princes. Ibid.
Prop. xxiii.

(*It must be borne in mind, that* "*Ecumenical Councils*" *here mean Roman Councils, not recognised by
the rest of the Church. The Councils of the early
Church did not interfere with the jurisdiction of the civil
power.*)

7. Or that the Church may not employ force.

(*Ecclesia vis inferendæ potestatem non habet.*)   'Syllabus,' Prop. xxiv.

8. Or that power, not inherent in the office of the
Episcopate, but granted to it by the civil authority,
may be withdrawn from it at the discretion of that
authority.   Ibid. Prop. xxv.

9. Or that the civil immunity (*immunitas*) of the
Church and its ministers, depends upon civil right.
Ibid. Prop. xxx.

10. Or that in the conflict of laws civil and
ecclesiastical, the civil law should prevail.   Ibid.
Prop. xlii.

11. Or that any method of instruction of youth,
solely secular, may be approved.   Ibid. Prop. xlviii.

12. Or that knowledge of things philosophical and
civil, may and should decline to be guided by Divine
and Ecclesiastical authority.   Ibid. Prop. lvii.

13. Or that marriage is not in its essence a Sacrament.   Ibid. Prop. lxvi.

14. Or that marriage, not sacramentally contracted,
(*si sacramentum excludatur*) has a binding force.   Ibid.
Prop. lxxiii.

15. Or that the abolition of the Temporal Power
of the Popedom would be highly advantageous to the
Church.   Ibid. Prop. lxxvi.   Also lxx.

16. Or that any other religion than the Roman
religion may be established by a State.   Ibid. Prop.
lxxvii.

17. Or that in " Countries called Catholic," the

c

free exercise of other religions may laudably be allowed. 'Syllabus,' Prop. lxxviii.

18. Or that the Roman Pontiff ought to come to terms with progress, liberalism, and modern civilization. Ibid. Prop. lxxx. *

This list is now perhaps sufficiently extended, although I have as yet not touched the decrees of 1870. But, before quitting it, I must offer three observations on what it contains.

Firstly. I do not place all the Propositions in one and the same category; for there are a portion of them which, as far as I can judge, might, by the combined aid of favourable construction and vigorous explanation, be brought within bounds. And I hold that favourable construction of the terms used in controversies is the right general rule. But this can only be so, when construction is an open question. When the author of certain propositions claims, as in the case before us, a sole and unlimited power to interpret them in such manner and by such rules as he may from time to time think fit, the only defence for all others concerned is at once to judge for themselves, how much of unreason or of mischief the words, naturally understood, may contain.

Secondly. It may appear, upon a hasty perusal, that neither the infliction of penalty in life, limb,

---

* For the original passages from the Encyclical and Syllabus of Pius IX., see Appendix A.

liberty, or goods, on disobedient members of the Christian Church, nor the title to depose sovereigns, and release subjects from their allegiance, with all its revolting consequences, has been here reaffirmed. In terms, there is no mention of them; but in the substance of the propositions, I grieve to say, they are beyond doubt included. For it is notorious that they have been declared and decreed by " Rome," that is to say by Popes and Papal Councils; and the stringent condemnations of the Syllabus include all those who hold that Popes and Papal Councils (declared ecumenical) have transgressed the just limits of their power, or usurped the rights of princes. What have been their opinions and decrees about persecution I need hardly say; and indeed the right to employ physical force is even here undisguisedly claimed (No. 7).

Even while I am writing, I am reminded, from an unquestionable source, of the words of Pope Pius IX. himself on the deposing power. I add only a few italics; the words appear as given in a translation, without the original :—

"The present Pontiff used these words in replying to the address from the Academia of the Catholic Religion (July 21, 1873) :—

"'There are many errors regarding the Infallibility: but the most malicious of all is that which includes, in that dogma, the *right* of deposing sovereigns, and declaring the people no longer bound by the obligation of fidelity. This *right* has now and again, in critical circumstances, been exercised by the Pontiffs: but it has nothing to do with Papal Infallibility. Its origin was not the infallibility, but the authority of the Pope. This authority, in accordance with public right, which was then vigorous, and with the acquiescence of all Christian nations, who reverenced in the Pope the supreme Judge of the Christian Commonwealth, *extended so far as to pass judgment, even in civil affairs, on the acts of Princes and of Nations.'* " *

Lastly. I must observe that these are not mere opinions of the Pope himself, nor even are they opinions which he might paternally recommend to the pious consideration of the faithful. With the promulgation of his opinions is unhappily combined, in the Encyclical Letter, which virtually, though not expressly, includes the whole, a command to all his spiritual children (from which command we the disobedient children are in no way excluded) to hold them.

"Itaque omnes et singulas pravas opiniones et doctrinas singillatim hisce literis commemoratas auctoritate nostrâ Apostolicâ reprobamus, proscribimus, atque damnamus; easque ab omnibus Catholicæ Ecclesiæ filiis, veluti reprobatas, proscriptas, atque damnatas omnino haberi volumus et mandamus." Encycl. Dec. 8, 1864.

And the decrees of 1870 will presently show us, what they establish as the binding force of the *mandate* thus conveyed to the Christian world.

---

* 'Civilization and the See of Rome.' By Lord Robert Montagu. Dublin, 1874. A Lecture delivered under the auspices of the Catholic Union of Ireland. I have a little misgiving about the version: but not of a nature to affect the substance.

IV. THE THIRD PROPOSITION.

I now pass to the operation of these extraordinary declarations on personal and private duty.

When the cup of endurance, which had so long been filling, began, with the council of the Vatican in 1870, to overflow, the most famous and learned living theologian of the Roman Communion, Dr. von Döllinger, long the foremost champion of his Church, refused compliance, and submitted, with his temper undisturbed and his freedom unimpaired, to the extreme and most painful penalty of excommunication. With him, many of the most learned and respected theologians of the Roman Communion in Germany underwent the same sentence. The very few, who elsewhere (I do not speak of Switzerland) suffered in like manner, deserve an admiration rising in proportion to their fewness. It seems as though Germany, from which Luther blew the mighty trumpet that even now echoes through the land, still retained her primacy in the domain of conscience, still supplied the *centuria prærogativa* of the great *comitia* of the world.

But let no man wonder or complain. Without imputing to anyone the moral murder, for such it is, of stifling conscience and conviction, I for one cannot be surprised that the fermentation, which is working through the mind of the Latin Church, has as yet (elsewhere than in Germany) but in few instances come to the surface. By the mass of mankind, it is

morally impossible that questions such as these can
be adequately examined; so it ever has been, and so
in the main it will continue, until the principles of
manufacturing machinery shall have been applied,
and with analogous results, to intellectual and moral
processes. Followers they are and must be, and in a
certain sense ought to be. But what as to the leaders
of society, the men of education and of leisure? I will
try to suggest some answer in few words. A change of
religious profession is under all circumstances a great
and awful thing. Much more is the question, however,
between conflicting, or apparently conflicting, duties
arduous, when the religion of a man has been changed
for him, over his head, and without the very least of
his participation. Far be it then from me to make any
Roman Catholic, except the great hierarchic Power,
and those who have egged it on, responsible for the
portentous proceedings which we have witnessed.
My conviction is that, even of those who may not shake
off the yoke, multitudes will vindicate at any rate their
loyalty at the expense of the consistency, which perhaps in difficult matters of religion few among us perfectly maintain. But this belongs to the future; for
the present, nothing could in my opinion be more
unjust than to hold the members of the Roman Church
in general already responsible for the recent innova-
tions. The duty of observers, who think the claims
involved in these decrees arrogant and false, and such
as not even impotence real or supposed ought to

shield from criticism, is frankly to state the case, and, by way of friendly challenge, to intreat their Roman Catholic fellow-countrymen to replace themselves in the position which five-and-forty years ago this nation, by the voice and action of its Parliament, declared its belief that they held.

Upon a strict re-examination of the language, as a part from the substance of my fourth Proposition, I find it faulty, inasmuch as it seems to imply that a "convert" now joining the Papal Church, not only gives up certain rights and duties of freedom, but surrenders them by a conscious and deliberate act. What I have less accurately said that he renounced, I might have more accurately said that he forfeited. To speak strictly, the claim now made upon him by the authority, which he solemnly and with the highest responsibility acknowledges, requires him to surrender his mental and moral freedom, and to place his loyalty and civil duty at the mercy of another. There may have been, and may be, persons who in their sanguine trust will not shrink from this result, and will console themselves with the notion that their loyalty and civil duty are to be committed to the custody of one much wiser than themselves. But I am sure that there are also "converts" who, when they perceive, will by word and act reject, the consequence which relentless logic draws for them. If, however, my proposition be true, there is no escape from the dilemma. Is it then true, or is it not true, that Rome requires a convert, who now joins her, to forfeit his moral and mental freedom, and to place his loyalty and civil duty at the mercy of another?

In order to place this matter in as clear a light as I can, it will be necessary to go back a little upon our recent history.

A century ago we began to relax that system of penal laws against Roman Catholics, at once petti-fogging, base, and cruel, which Mr. Burke has scathed and blasted with his immortal eloquence.

When this process had reached the point, at which the question was whether they should be admitted into Parliament, there arose a great and prolonged national controversy; and some men, who at no time of their lives were narrow-minded, such as Sir Robert Peel, the Minister, resisted the concession. The arguments in its favour were obvious and strong, and they ultimately prevailed. But the strength of the opposing party had lain in the allegation that, from the nature and claims of the Papal power, it was not possible for the consistent Roman Catholic to pay to the crown of this country an entire allegiance, and that the admission of persons, thus self-disabled, to Parliament was inconsistent with the safety of the State and nation; which had not very long before, it may be observed, emerged from a struggle for existence.

An answer to this argument was indispensable; and it was supplied mainly from two sources. The

Josephine laws,* then still subsisting in the Austrian empire, and the arrangements which had been made after the peace of 1815 by Prussia and the German States with Pius VII. and Gonsalvi, proved that the Papal Court could submit to circumstances, and could allow material restraints even upon the exercise of its ecclesiastical prerogatives. Here, then, was a reply in the sense of the phrase *solvitur ambulando.* Much information of this class was collected for the information of Parliament and the country.† But there were also measures taken to learn, from the highest Roman Catholic authorities of this country, what was the exact situation of the members of that communion with respect to some of the better known exorbitancies of Papal assumption. Did the Pope claim any temporal jurisdiction? Did he still pretend to the exercise of a power to depose kings, release subjects from their allegiance, and incite them to revolt? Was faith to be kept with heretics? Did the Church still teach the doctrines of persecution? Now, to no

---

* See the work of Count dal Pozzo on the 'Austrian Ecclesiastical Law.' London: Murray, 1827. The Leopoldine Laws in Tuscany may also be mentioned.

† See ' Report from the Select Committee appointed to report the nature and substance of the Laws and Ordinances existing in Foreign States, respecting the regulation of their Roman Catholic subjects in Ecclesiastical matters, and their intercourse with the See of Rome, or any other Foreign Ecclesiastical Jurisdiction.' Printed for the House of Commons in 1816 and 1817. Reprinted 1851.

one of these questions could the answer really be of the smallest immediate moment to this powerful and solidly compacted kingdom. They were topics selected by way of sample; and the intention was to elicit declarations showing generally that the fangs of the mediæval Popedom had been drawn, and its claws torn away; that the Roman system, however strict in its dogma, was perfectly compatible with civil liberty, and with the institutions of a free State moulded on a different religious basis from its own.

Answers in abundance were obtained, tending to show that the doctrines of deposition and persecution, of keeping no faith with heretics, and of universal dominion, were obsolete beyond revival; that every assurance could be given respecting them, except such as required the shame of a formal retractation; that they were in effect mere bugbears, unworthy to be taken into account by a nation, which prided itself on being made up of practical men.

But it was unquestionably felt that something more than the renunciation of these particular opinions was necessary in order to secure the full concession of civil rights to Roman Catholics. As to their individual loyalty, a State disposed to generous or candid interpretation had no reason to be uneasy. It was only with regard to requisitions, which might be made on them from another quarter, that apprehension could exist. It was reasonable that England should desire to know not only what the Pope* might do for himself, but to what demands, by the constitution of their Church, they were liable; and how far it was possible that such demands could touch their civil duty. The theory which placed every human being, in things spiritual and things temporal, at the feet of the Roman Pontiff, had not been an *idolum specûs*, a mere theory of the chamber. Brain-power never surpassed in the political history of the world had been devoted for centuries to the single purpose of working it into the practice of Christendom; had in the West achieved for an impossible problem a partial success; and had in the East punished the obstinate independence of the Church by that Latin conquest of Constantinople, which effectually prepared the way for the downfall of the Eastern empire, and the establishment of the Turks in Europe. What was really material therefore was, not whether the Papal chair laid claim to this or that particular power, but whether it laid claim to some power that included them all, and whether that claim had received such sanction from the authorities of the Latin Church, that there remained within her borders

---

* At that period the eminent and able Bishop Doyle did not scruple to write as follows : " We are taunted with the proceedings of Popes. What, my Lord, have we Catholics to do with the proceedings of Popes, or why should we be made accountable for them ?"—' Essay on the Catholic Claims.' To Lord Liverpool, 1826, p. 111.

absolutely no tenable standing-ground from which war against it could be maintained. Did the Pope then claim infallibility? Or did he, either without infallibility or with it (and if with it so much the worse), claim an universal obedience from his flock? And were these claims, either or both, affirmed in his Church by authority which even the least Papal of the members of that Church must admit to be binding upon conscience?

The two first of these questions were covered by the third. And well it was that they were so covered. For to them no satisfactory answer could even then be given. The Popes had kept up, with comparatively little intermission, for well-nigh a thousand years their claim to dogmatic infallibility; and had, at periods within the same tract of time, often enough made, and never retracted, that other claim which is theoretically less but practically larger; their claim to an obedience virtually universal from the baptised members of the Church. To the third question it was fortunately more practicable to prescribe a satisfactory reply. It was well known that, in the days of its glory and intellectual power, the great Gallican Church had not only not admitted, but had denied Papal infallibility, and had declared that the local laws and usages of the Church could not be set aside by the will of the Pontiff. Nay, further, it was believed that in the main these had been, down to the close of the last century, the prevailing opinions of the Cisalpine Churches in communion with Rome. The Council of Constance had in act as well as word shown that the Pope's judgments, and the Pope himself, were triable by the assembled representatives of the Christian world. And the Council of Trent, notwithstanding the predominance in it of Italian and Roman influences, if it had not denied, yet had not affirmed either proposition.

All that remained was, to know what were the sentiments entertained on these vital points by the leaders and guides of Roman Catholic opinion nearest to our own doors. And here testimony was offered, which must not, and cannot, be forgotten. In part, this was the testimony of witnesses before the Committees of the two Houses in 1824 and 1825. I need quote two answers only, given by the Prelate, who more than any other represented his Church, and influenced the mind of this country in favour of concession at the time, namely, Bishop Doyle. He was asked,*

" In what, and how far, does the Roman Catholic profess to obey the Pope ? "

------

* Committees of both Lords and Commons sat ; the former in 1825, the latter in 1824-5. The References were identical, and ran as follows : " To inquire into the state of Ireland, more particularly with reference to the circumstances which may have led to disturbances in that part of the United Kingdom." Bishop Doyle was examined March 21, 1825, and April 21, 1825, before the Lords. The two citations in the text are taken from Bishop Doyle's evidence before the Commons' Committee, March 12, 1825, p. 190.

He replied :

" The Catholic professes to obey the Pope in matters which regard his religious faith : and in those matters of ecclesiastical discipline which have already been defined by the competent authorities."

And again.

" Does that justify the objection that is made to Catholics, that their allegiance is divided ? "

" I do not think it does in any way. We are bound to obey the Pope in those things that I have already mentioned. But our obedience to the law, and the allegiance which we owe the sovereign, are complete, and full, and perfect, and undivided, inasmuch as they extend to all political, legal, and civil rights of the king or of his subjects. I think the allegiance due to the king, and the allegiance due to the Pope, are as distinct and as divided in their nature, as any two things can possibly be."

Such is the opinion of the dead Prelate. We shall presently hear the opinion of a living one. But the sentiments of the dead man powerfully operated on the open and trustful temper of this people to induce them to grant, at the cost of so much popular feeling and national tradition, the great and just concession of 1829. That concession, without such declarations, it would, to say the least, have been far more difficult to obtain.

Now, bodies are usually held to be bound by the evidence of their own selected and typical witnesses. But in this instance the colleagues of those witnesses thought fit also to speak collectively.

First let us quote from the collective " Declaration," in the year 1826, of the Vicars Apostolic, who, with Episcopal authority, governed the Roman Catholics of Great Britain.

" The allegiance which Catholics hold to be due, and are bound to pay, to their Sovereign, and to the civil authority of the State, is perfect and undivided. . . . .

" They declare that neither the Pope, nor any other prelate or ecclesiastical person of the Roman Catholic Church . . . . has any right to interfere directly or indirectly in the Civil Government . . . . nor to oppose in any manner the performance of the civil duties which are due to the king."

Not less explicit was the Hierarchy of the Roman Communion in its " Pastoral Address to the Clergy and Laity of the Roman Catholic Church in Ireland," dated January 25, 1826. This address contains a Declaration, from which I extract the following words :—

" It is a duty which they owe to themselves, *as well as to their Protestant fellow-subjects*, whose good opinion they value, to endeavour once more to remove the false imputations that have been frequently cast upon the faith and discipline of that Church which is intrusted to their care, *that all may be enabled to know with accuracy their genuine principles*."

In Article 11 :—

" They declare on oath their belief that it is not an article of the Catholic Faith, neither are they thereby required to believe, that the Pope is infallible."

and, after various recitals, they set forth

" After this full, explicit, and sworn declaration, we are utterly at a loss to conceive on what possible ground we could be justly charged with bearing towards our most gracious Sovereign only a divided allegiance."

Thus, besides much else that I will not stop to quote,

Papal infallibility was most solemnly declared to be a matter on which each man might think as he pleased; the Pope's power to claim obedience was strictly and narrowly limited : it was expressly denied that he had any title, direct or indirect, to interfere in civil government. Of the right of the Pope to define the limits which divide the civil from the spiritual by his own authority, not one word is said by the Prelates of either country.

Since that time, all these propositions have been reversed. The Pope's infallibility, when he speaks *ex cathedrâ* on faith and morals, has been declared, with the assent of the Bishops of the Roman Church, to be an article of faith, binding on the conscience of every Christian; his claim to the obedience of his spiritual subjects has been declared in like manner without any practical limit or reserve; and his supremacy, without any reserve of civil rights, has been similarly affirmed to include everything which relates to the discipline and government of the Church throughout the world. And these doctrines, we now know on the highest authority, it is of necessity for salvation to believe.

Independently, however, of the Vatican Decrees themselves, it is necessary for all who wish to understand what has been the amount of the wonderful change now consummated in the constitution of the Latin Church, and what is the present degradation of its Episcopal order, to observe also the change, amounting to revolution, of form in the present, as compared with other conciliatory decrees. Indeed, that spirit of centralisation, the excesses of which are as fatal to vigorous life in the Church as in the State, seems now nearly to have reached the last and furthest point of possible advancement and exaltation.

When, in fact, we speak of the decrees of the Council of the Vatican, we use a phrase which will not bear strict examination. The Canons of the Council of Trent were, at least, the real Canons of a real Council: and the strain in which they are promulgated is this :—*Hæc sacrosancta, ecumenica, et generalis Tridentina Synodus, in Spiritu Sancto legitimè congregata, in eâ præsidentibus eisdem tribus apostolicis Legatis, hortatur,* or *docet,* or *statuit,* or *decernit,* and the like: and its canons, as published in Rome, are "*Canones et decreta Sacrosancti ecumenici Concilii Tridentini,*"* and so forth. But what we have now to do with is the *Constitutio Dogmatica Prima de Ecclesiâ Christi, edita in Sessione tertiâ* of the Vatican Council. It is not a constitution made by the Council, but one promulgated in the Council.† And who is it that legislates and decrees? It is *Pius Episcopus, servus*

---

* 'Romæ : in Collegio urbano de Propagandâ Fide.' 1833.

† I am aware that, as some hold, this was the case with the Council of the Lateran in A.D. 1215. But, first, this has not been established : secondly, the very gist of the evil we are dealing with consists in following (and enforcing) precedents from the age of Pope Innocent III.

servorum Dei: and the seductive plural of his *docemus
et declaramus* is simply the dignified and ceremonious
"We" of Royal declarations. The document is
dated *Pontificatûs nostri Anno XXV*: and the humble
share of the assembled Episcopate in the transaction
is represented by *sacro approbante concilio*. And now
for the propositions themselves.

First comes the Pope's infallibility:—

"Docemus, et divinitus revelatum dogma esse definimus,
Romanum Pontificem, cum ex Cathedrâ loquitur, id est cum,
omnium Christianorum Pastoris et Doctoris munere fungens,
pro supremâ suâ Apostolicâ auctoritate doctrinam de fide vel
moribus ab universâ Ecclesiâ tenendam definit, per assistentiam
divinam, ipsi in Beato Petro promissam, eâ infallibilitate pollere,
quâ Divinus Redemptor Ecclesiam suam in definiendâ doctrinâ
de fide vel moribus instructam esse voluit: ideoque ejus Romani
Pontificis definitiones ex sese non autem ex consensu Ecclesiæ
irreformabiles esse."*

Will it, then, be said that the infallibility of the
Pope accrues only when he speaks *ex cathedrâ*? No
doubt this is a very material consideration for those,
who have been told that the private conscience is to
derive comfort and assurance from the emanations
of the Papal Chair: for there is no established or
accepted definition of the phrase *ex cathedrâ*, and he
has no power to obtain one, and no guide to direct
him in his choice among some twelve theories on
the subject, which, it is said, are bandied to and fro

---

* 'Constitutio de Ecclesiâ,' c. iv.

among Roman theologians, except the despised and discarded agency of his private judgment. But while thus sorely tantalised, he is not one whit protected. For there is still one person, and one only, who can unquestionably declare *ex cathedrâ* what is *ex cathedrâ* and what is not, and who can declare it when and as he pleases. That person is the Pope himself. The provision is, that no document he issues shall be valid without a seal: but the seal remains under his own sole lock and key.

Again, it may be sought to plead, that the Pope is, after all, only operating by sanctions which unquestionably belong to the religious domain. He does not propose to invade the country, to seize Woolwich, or burn Portsmouth. He will only, at the worst, excommunicate opponents, as he has excommunicated Dr. von Döllinger and others. Is this a good answer? After all, even in the Middle Ages, it was not by the direct action of fleets and armies of their own that the Popes contended with kings who were refractory; it was mainly by interdicts, and by the refusal, which they entailed when the Bishops were not brave enough to refuse their publication, of religious offices to the people. It was thus that England suffered under John, France under Philip Augustus, Leon under Alphonso the Noble, and every country in its turn. But the inference may be drawn that they who, while using spiritual weapons for such an end, do not employ temporal means, only

D 2

fail to employ them because they have them not.
A religious society, which delivers volleys of spiritual
censures in order to impede the performance of
civil duties, does all the mischief that is in its power
to do, and brings into question, in the face of the
State, its title to civil protection.

Will it be said, finally, that the Infallibility touches
only matter of faith and morals? Only matter of
morals! Will any of the Roman casuists kindly
acquaint us what are the departments and functions
of human life which do not and cannot fall within the
domain of morals? If they will not tell us, we must
look elsewhere. In his work entitled 'Literature
and Dogma,'* Mr. Matthew Arnold quaintly informs
us—as they tell us nowadays how many parts of our
poor bodies are solid, and how many aqueous—that
about seventy-five per cent. of all we do belongs to
the department of "conduct." Conduct and morals,
we may suppose, are nearly co-extensive. Three-
fourths, then, of life are thus handed over. But who
will guarantee to us the other fourth? Certainly
not St. Paul; who says, "Whether therefore ye eat,
or drink, or whatsoever ye do, do *all* to the glory of
God." And "Whatsoever ye do, in word or in
deed, do *all* in the name of the Lord Jesus."† No!
Such a distinction would be the unworthy device of a

---

* Pages 15, 44.
† 1 Cor. x. 31; Col. iii. 7.

shallow policy, vainly used to hide the daring of that wild ambition which at Rome, not from the throne but from behind the throne, prompts the movements of the Vatican. I care not to ask if there be dregs or tatters of human life, such as can escape from the description and boundary of morals. I submit that Duty is a power which rises with us in the morning, and goes to rest with us at night. It is co-extensive with the action of our intelligence. It is the shadow which cleaves to us go where we will, and which only leaves us when we leave the light of life. So then it is the supreme direction of us in respect to all Duty, which the Pontiff declares to belong to him, *sacro approbante concilio:* and this declaration he makes, not as an otiose opinion of the schools, but *cunctis fidelibus credendam et tenendam.*

But we shall now see that, even if a loophole had at this point been left unclosed, the void is supplied by another provision of the Decrees. While the reach of the Infallibility is as wide as it may please the Pope, or those who may prompt the Pope, to make it, there is something wider still, and that is the claim to an absolute and entire Obedience. This Obedience is to be rendered to his orders in the cases I shall proceed to point out, without any qualifying condition, such as the *ex cathedrâ.* The sounding name of Infallibility has so fascinated the public mind, and riveted it on the Fourth Chapter of the Constitution *de Ecclesiâ,* that its near neighbour, the

Third Chapter, has, at least in my opinion, received very much less than justice. Let us turn to it.

" Cujuscunque ritûs et dignitatis pastores atque fideles, tam seorsum singuli quam simul omnes, officio hierarchicæ subordinationis veræque obedientiæ obstringuntur, non solum in rebus, quæ ad fidem et mores, sed etiam in iis, quæ ad disciplinam et regimen Ecclesiæ per totum orbem diffusæ pertinent. . . . . Hæc est Catholicæ veritatis doctrina, a quâ deviare, salvâ fide atque salute, nemo potest. . . .

" Docemus etiam et declaramus eum esse judicem supremum fidelium, et in omnibus causis ad examen ecclesiasticum spectantibus ad ipsius posse judicium recurri : Sedis vero Apostolicæ, cujus auctoritate major non est, judicium a nemine fore retractandum. Neque cuiquam de ejus licere judicare judicio."*

Even, therefore, where the judgments of the Pope do not present the credentials of infallibility, they are unappealable and irreversible : no person may pass judgment upon them ; and all men, clerical and lay, dispersedly or in the aggregate, are bound truly to obey them ; and from this rule of Catholic truth no man can depart, save at the peril of his salvation. Surely, it is allowable to say that this Third Chapter on universal obedience is a formidable rival to the Fourth Chapter on Infallibility. Indeed, to an observer from without, it seems to leave the dignity to the other, but to reserve the stringency and efficiency to itself. The Fourth Chapter is the Merovingian Monarch ; the third is the Carolingian Mayor of the Palace. The fourth has an overawing splendour ;

* ' Dogmatic Constitutions,' &c., c. iii.   Dublin, 1870, pp. 30-32.

the third, an iron gripe. Little does it matter to me
whether my superior claims infallibility, so long as
he is entitled to demand and exact conformity. This,
it will be observed, he demands even in cases not
covered by his infallibility ; cases, therefore, in which
he admits it to be possible that he may be wrong, but
finds it intolerable to be told so. As he must be
obeyed in all his judgments though not *ex cathedrâ*,
it seems a pity he could not likewise give the com-
forting assurance that, they are all certain to be
right.

But why this ostensible reduplication, this apparent surplusage ? Why did the astute contrivers of
this tangled scheme conclude that they could not
afford to rest content with pledging the Council to
Infallibility in terms which are not only wide to a
high degree, but elastic beyond all measure ?

Though they must have known perfectly well that
" faith and morals " carried everything, or everything
worth having, in the purely individual sphere, they
also knew just as well that, even where the individual
was subjugated, they might and would still have to
deal with the State.

In mediæval history, this distinction is not only
clear, but glaring. Outside the borders of some
narrow and proscribed sect, now and then emerging,
we never, or scarcely ever, hear of private and personal resistance to the Pope. The manful " Protestantism " of mediæval times had its activity almost

entirely in the sphere of public, national, and state rights. Too much attention, in my opinion, cannot be fastened on this point. It is the very root and kernel of the matter. Individual servitude, however abject, will not satisfy the party now dominant in the Latin Church: the State must also be a slave.

Our Saviour had recognised as distinct the two provinces of the civil rule and the Church : had nowhere intimated that the spiritual authority was to claim the disposal of physical force, and to control in its own domain the authority which is alone responsible for external peace, order, and safety among civilised communities of men. It has been alike the peculiarity, the pride, and the misfortune of the Roman Church, among Christian communities, to allow to itself an unbounded use, as far as its power would go, of earthly instruments for spiritual ends. We have seen with what ample assurances* this nation and Parliament were fed in 1826 ; how well and roundly the full and undivided rights of the civil power, and the separation of the two jurisdictions, were affirmed. All this had at length been undone, as far as Popes could undo it, in the Syllabus and the Encyclical. It remained to complete the undoing, through the subserviency or pliability of the Council.

And the work is now truly complete. Lest it

---

* See further, Appendix B.

should be said that supremacy in faith and morals, full dominion over personal belief and conduct, did not cover the collective action of men in States, a third province was opened, not indeed to the abstract assertion of Infallibility, but to the far more practical and decisive demand of absolute Obedience. And this is the proper work of the Third Chapter, to which I am endeavouring to do a tardy justice. Let us listen again to its few but pregnant words on the point :

" Non solum in rebus, quæ ad fidem et mores, sed etiam in iis, quæ ad disciplinam et regimen Ecclesiæ per totum orbem diffusæ pertinent."

Absolute obedience, it is boldly declared, is due to the Pope, at the peril of salvation, not alone in faith, in morals, but in all things which concern the discipline and government of the Church. Thus are swept into the Papal net whole multitudes of facts, whole systems of government, prevailing, though in different degrees, in every country of the world. Even in the United States, where the severance between Church and State is supposed to be complete, a long catalogue might be drawn of subjects belonging to the domain and competency of the State, but also undeniably affecting the government of the Church; such as, by way of example, marriage, burial, education, prison discipline, blasphemy, poor-relief, incorporation, mortmain, religious endowments, vows of celibacy and obedience. In Europe the circle is far wider, the points of contact and of interlacing almost innumerable. But on all matters, respecting which any Pope may think proper to declare that they concern either faith, or morals, or the government or discipline of the Church, he claims, with the approval of a Council undoubtedly Ecumenical in the Roman sense, the absolute obedience, at the peril of salvation, of every member of his communion.

It seems not as yet to have been thought wise to pledge the Council in terms to the Syllabus and the Encyclical. That achievement is probably reserved for some one of its sittings yet to come. In the meantime it is well to remember, that this claim in respect of all things affecting the discipline and government of the Church, as well as faith and conduct, is lodged in open day by and in the reign of a Pontiff, who has condemned free speech, free writing, a free press, toleration of nonconformity, liberty of conscience, the study of civil and philosophical matters in independence of the ecclesiastical authority, marriage unless sacramentally contracted, and the definition by the State of the civil rights (*jura*) of the Church; who has demanded for the Church, therefore, the title to define its own civil rights, together with a divine right to civil immunities, and a right to use physical force; and who has also proudly asserted that the Popes of the Middle Ages with their councils did not invade the rights of princes: as for example, Gregory VII., of the Emperor

Henry IV.; Innocent III., of Raymond of Toulouse; Paul III., in deposing Henry VIII.; or Pius V., in performing the like paternal office for Elizabeth.

I submit, then, that my fourth proposition is true: and that England is entitled to ask, and to know, in what way the obedience required by the Pope and the Council of the Vatican is to be reconciled with the integrity of civil allegiance?

It has been shown that the Head of their Church, so supported as undoubtedly to speak with its highest authority, claims from Roman Catholics a plenary obedience to whatever he may desire in relation not to faith but to morals, and not only to these, but to all that concerns the government and discipline of the Church : that, of this, much lies within the domain of the State : that, to obviate all misapprehension, the Pope demands for himself the right to determine the province of his own rights, and has so defined it in formal documents, as to warrant any and every invasion of the civil sphere ; and that this new version of the principles of the Papal Church inexorably binds its members to the admission of these exorbitant claims, without any refuge or reservation on behalf of their duty to the Crown.

Under circumstances such as these, it seems not too much to ask of them to confirm the opinion which we, as fellow-countrymen, entertain of them, by sweeping away, in such manner and terms as they may think best, the presumptive imputations which

their ecclesiastical rulers at Rome, acting autocrati-
cally, appear to have brought upon their capacity to
pay a solid and undivided allegiance ; and to fulfil
the engagement which their Bishops, as political
sponsors, promised and declared for them in 1825.

It would be impertinent, as well as needless, to
suggest what should be said. All that is requisite is
to indicate in substance that which (if the foregoing
argument be sound) is not wanted, and that which
is. What is not wanted is vague and general assertion, of whatever kind, and however sincere. What
is wanted, and that in the most specific form and
the clearest terms, I take to be one of two things;
that is to say, either—

I. A demonstration that neither in the name of
faith, nor in the name of morals, nor in the name of
the government or discipline of the Church, is the
Pope of Rome able, by virtue of the powers asserted
for him by the Vatican decree, to make any claim
upon those who adhere to his communion, of such a
nature as can impair the integrity of their civil
allegiance ; or else,

II. That, if and when such claim is made, it will
even although resting on the definitions of the
Vatican, be repelled and rejected; just as Bishop
Doyle, when he was asked what the Roman Catholic
clergy would do if the Pope intermeddled with their
religion, replied frankly, " The consequence would
be, that we should oppose him by every means in

our power, even by the exercise of our spiritual authority." *

In the absence of explicit assurances to this effect, we should appear to be led, nay, driven, by just reasoning upon that documentary evidence, to the conclusions:—

1. That the Pope, authorised by his Council, claims for himself the domain (*a*) of faith, (*b*) of morals, (*c*) of all that concerns the government and discipline of the Church.

2. That he in like manner claims the power of determining the limits of those domains.

3. That he does not sever them, by any acknowledged or intelligible line, from the domains of civil duty and allegiance.

4. That he therefore claims, and claims from the month of July 1870 onwards with plenary authority, from every convert and member of his Church, that he shall "place his loyalty and civil duty at the mercy of another:" that other being himself.

V. BEING TRUE, ARE THE PROPOSITIONS MATERIAL?

But next, if these propositions be true, are they also material? The claims cannot, as I much fear, be denied to have been made. It cannot be denied that the Bishops, who govern in things spiritual more

---

* ' Report,' March 18, 1826, p. 191.

than five millions (or nearly one-sixth) of the inhabitants of the United Kingdom, have in some cases promoted, in all cases accepted, these claims. It has been a favourite purpose of my life not to conjure up, but to conjure down, public alarms. I am not now going to pretend that either foreign foe or domestic treason can, at the bidding of the Court of Rome, disturb these peaceful shores. But though such fears may be visionary, it is more visionary still to suppose for one moment that the claims of Gregory VII., of Innocent III., and of Boniface VIII., have been disinterred, in the nineteenth century, like hideous mummies picked out of Egyptian sarcophagi, in the interests of archæology, or without a definite and practical aim. As rational beings, we must rest assured that only with a very clearly conceived and foregone purpose have these astonishing reassertions been paraded before the world. What is that purpose?

I can well believe that it is in part theological. There have always been, and there still are, no small proportion of our race, and those by no means in all respects the worst, who are sorely open to the temptation, especially in times of religious disturbance, to discharge their spiritual responsibilities by *power of attorney*. As advertising Houses find custom in proportion, not so much to the solidity of their resources as to the magniloquence of their promises and assurances, so theological boldness in the extension of such claims is sure to pay, by widening certain circles of devoted adherents, however it may repel the mass of mankind. There were two special encouragements to this enterprise at the present day : one of them the perhaps unconscious but manifest leaning of some, outside the Roman precinct, to undue exaltation of Church power; the other the reaction, which is and must be brought about in favour of superstition, by the levity of the destructive speculations so widely current, and the notable hardihood of the anti-Christian writing of the day.

But it is impossible to account sufficiently in this manner for the particular course which has been actually pursued by the Roman Court. All morbid spiritual appetites would have been amply satisfied by claims to infallibility in creed, to the prerogative of miracle, to dominion over the unseen world. In truth there was occasion, in this view, for nothing, except a liberal supply of Salmonean thunder :—

" Dum flammas Jovis, et sonitus imitatur Olympi."*

All this could have been managed by a few Tetzels, judiciously distributed over Europe. Therefore the question still remains, Why did that Court, with policy for ever in its eye, lodge such formidable demands for power of the vulgar kind in that sphere which is visible, and where hard knocks can undoubtedly be given as well as received ?

* Æn. vi. 586.

It must be for some political object, of a very tangible kind, that the risks of so daring a raid upon the civil sphere have been deliberately run.

A daring raid it is. For it is most evident that the very assertion of principles which establish an exemption from allegiance, or which impair its completeness, goes, in many other countries of Europe, far more directly than with us, to the creation of political strife, and to dangers of the most material and tangible kind. The struggle, now proceeding in Germany, at once occurs to the mind as a palmary instance. I am not competent to give any opinion upon the particulars of that struggle. The institutions of Germany, and the relative estimate of State power and individual freedom, are materially different from ours. But I must say as much as this. First, it is not Prussia alone that is touched; elsewhere, too, the bone lies ready, though the contention may be delayed. In other States, in Austria particularly, there are recent laws in force, raising much the same issues as the Falck laws have raised. But the Roman Court possesses in perfection one art, the art of waiting; and it is her wise maxim to fight but one enemy at a time. Secondly, if I have truly represented the claims promulgated from the Vatican, it is difficult to deny that those claims, and the power which has made them, are primarily responsible for the pains and perils, whatever they may be, of the present conflict between German and Roman enactments. And that which was once truly said of France, may now also be said with not less truth of Germany: when Germany is disquieted, Europe cannot be at rest.

I should feel less anxiety on this subject had the Supreme Pontiff frankly recognised his altered position since the events of 1870; and, in language as clear, if not as emphatic, as that in which he has proscribed modern civilisation, given to Europe the assurance that he would be no party to the re-establishment by blood and violence of the Temporal Power of the Church. It is easy to conceive that his personal benevolence, no less than his feelings as an Italian, must have inclined him individually towards a course so humane; and I should add, if I might do it without presumption, so prudent. With what appears to an English eye a lavish prodigality, successive Italian Governments have made over the ecclesiastical powers and privileges of the Monarchy, not to the Church of the country for the revival of the ancient, popular, and self-governing elements of its constitution, but to the Papal Chair, for the establishment of ecclesiastical despotism, and the suppression of the last vestiges of independence. This course, so difficult for a foreigner to appreciate, or even to justify, has been met, not by reciprocal conciliation, but by a constant fire of denunciations and complaints. When the tone of these denunciations and complaints is compared

E

with the language of the authorised and favoured Papal organs in the press, and of the Ultramontane party (now the sole legitimate party of the Latin Church) throughout Europe, it leads many to the painful and revolting conclusion that there is a fixed purpose among the secret inspirers of Roman policy to pursue, by the road of force, upon the arrival of any favourable opportunity, the favourite project of re-erecting the terrestrial throne of the Popedom, even if it can only be re-erected on the ashes of the city, and amidst the whitening bones of the people.*

It is difficult to conceive or contemplate the effects of such an endeavour. But the existence at this day of the policy, even in bare idea, is itself a portentous evil. I do not hesitate to say that it is an incentive to general disturbance, a premium upon European wars. It is in my opinion not sanguine only, but almost ridiculous to imagine that such a project could eventually succeed; but it is difficult to over-estimate the effect which it might produce in generating and exasperating strife. It might even, to some extent, disturb and paralyse the action of such Governments as might interpose for no separate purpose of their own, but only with a view to the maintenance or restoration of the general peace. If the baleful Power which is expressed by the phrase *Curia Romana*, and not at all adequately rendered in its

---

* Appendix C.

historic force by the usual English equivalent
" Court of Rome," really entertains the scheme, it
doubtless counts on the support in every country of
an organised and devoted party ; which, when it can
command the scales of political power, will promote
interference, and, when it is in a minority, will work
for securing neutrality. As the peace of Europe
may be in jeopardy, and as the duties even of England, as one (so to speak) of its constabulary authorities, might come to be in question, it would be most
interesting to know the mental attitude of our Roman
Catholic fellow-countrymen in England and Ireland
with reference to the subject ; and it seems to be one,
on which we are entitled to solicit information.

For there cannot be the smallest doubt that the
temporal power of the Popedom comes within the
true meaning of the words used at the Vatican to
describe the subjects on which the Pope is authorised
to claim, under awful sanctions, the obedience of the
" faithful."   It is even possible that we have here
the key to the enlargement of the province of
Obedience beyond the limits of Infallibility, and to
the introduction of the remarkable phrase *ad disciplinam et regimen Ecclesiæ*. No impartial person can
deny that the question of the temporal power very
evidently concerns the discipline and government of
the Church—concerns it, and most mischievously as
I should venture to think ; but in the opinion, up to
a late date, of many Roman Catholics, not only most

E 2

beneficially, but even essentially. Let it be remembered, that such a man as the late Count Montalembert, who in his general politics was of the Liberal party, did not scruple to hold that the millions of Roman Catholics throughout the world were co-partners with the inhabitants of the States of the Church in regard to their civil government; and, as constituting the vast majority, were of course entitled to override them. It was also rather commonly held, a quarter of a century ago, that the question of the States of the Church was one with which none but Roman Catholic Powers could have anything to do. This doctrine, I must own, was to me at all times unintelligible. It is now, to say the least, hopelessly and irrecoverably obsolete.

Archbishop Manning, who is the head of the Papal Church in England, and whose ecclesiastical tone is supposed to be in the closest accordance with that of his headquarters, has not thought it too much to say that the civil order of all Christendom is the offspring of the Temporal Power, and has the Temporal Power for its keystone; that on the destruction of the Temporal Power "the laws of nations would at once fall in ruins;" that (our old friend) the deposing Power "taught subjects obedience and princes clemency."* Nay, this high

* 'Three Lectures on the Temporal Sovereignty of the Popes,' 1860, pp. 34, 46, 47, 58-9, 63.

authority has proceeded further; and has elevated the Temporal Power to the rank of necessary doctrine.

" The Catholic Church cannot be silent, it cannot hold its peace; it cannot cease to preach the doctrines of Revelation, not only of the Trinity and of the Incarnation, but likewise of the Seven Sacraments, and of the Infallibility of the Church of God, and of the necessity of Unity, and of the Sovereignty, both spiritual and temporal, of the Holy See." *

I never, for my own part, heard that the work containing this remarkable passage was placed in the ' Index Prohibitorum Librorum.' On the contrary, its distinguished author was elevated, on the first opportunity, to the headship of the Roman Episcopacy in England, and to the guidance of the million or thereabouts of souls in its communion. And the more recent utterances of the oracle have not descended from the high level of those already cited. They have, indeed, the recommendation of a comment, not without fair claims to authority, on the recent declarations of the Pope and the Council; and of one which goes to prove how far I am from having exaggerated or strained in the foregoing pages the meaning of those declarations. Especially does this hold good on the one point, the most vital of the whole— the title to define the border line of the two provinces, which the Archbishop not unfairly takes to be the true

---

* ' The present Crisis of the Holy See.' By H. E. Manning, D.D.   London, 1861, p. 73.

criterion of supremacy, as between rival powers like the Church and the State.

"If, then, the civil power be not competent to decide the limits of the spiritual power, and if the spiritual power can define, with a divine certainty, its own limits, it is evidently supreme. Or, in other words, the spiritual power knows, with divine certainty, the limits of its own jurisdiction : and it knows therefore the limits and the competence of the civil power. It is thereby, in matters of religion and conscience, supreme. I do not see how this can be denied without denying Christianity. And if this be so, this is the doctrine of the Bull *Unam Sanctam*,* and of the Syllabus, and of the Vatican Council. It is, in fact, Ultramontanism, for this term means neither less nor more. The Church, therefore, is separate and supreme.

"Let us then ascertain somewhat further, what is the meaning of supreme. Any power which is independent, *and can alone fix the limits of its own jurisdiction, and can thereby fix the limits of all other jurisdictions, is,* ipso facto, *supreme.*† But the Church of Jesus Christ, within the sphere of revelation, of faith and morals, is all this, or is nothing, or worse than nothing, an imposture and an usurpation—that is, it is Christ or Antichrist." ‡

But the whole pamphlet should be read by those who desire to know the true sense of the Papal declarations and Vatican decrees, as they are understood by the most favoured ecclesiastics ; understood, I am bound to own, so far as I can see, in their natural, legitimate, and inevitable sense. Such readers will

---

* On the Bull *Unam Sanctam*, "of a most odious kind;" see Bishop Doyle's Essay, already cited. He thus describes it.

† The italics are not in the original.

‡ 'Cæsarism and Ultramontanism.' By Archbishop Manning, 1874, pp. 35–6.

be assisted by the treatise in seeing clearly, and in admitting frankly that, whatever demands may hereafter, and in whatever circumstances, be made upon us, we shall be unable to advance with any fairness the plea that it has been done without due notice.

There are millions upon millions of the Protestants of this country, who would agree with Archbishop Manning, if he were simply telling us that Divine truth is not to be sought from the lips of the State, nor to be sacrificed at its command. But those millions would tell him, in return, that the State, as the power which is alone responsible for the external order of the world, can alone conclusively and finally be competent to determine what is to take place in the sphere of that external order.

I have shown, then, that the Propositions, especially that which has been felt to be the chief one among them, being true, are also material; material to be generally known, and clearly understood, and well considered, on civil grounds; inasmuch as they invade, at a multitude of points, the civil sphere, and seem even to have no very remote or shadowy connection with the future peace and security of Christendom.

VI. Were the Propositions proper to be set forth by the present Writer?

There remains yet before us only the shortest and least significant portion of the inquiry, namely, whether these things, being true, and being material to be said, were also proper to be said by me. I must ask pardon, if a tone of egotism be detected in this necessarily subordinate portion of my remarks.

For thirty years, and in a great variety of circumstances, in office and as an independent Member of Parliament, in majorities and in small minorities, and during the larger portion of the time * as the representative of a great constituency, mainly clerical, I have, with others, laboured to maintain and extend the civil rights of my Roman Catholic fellow-countrymen. The Liberal party of this country, with which I have been commonly associated, has suffered, and sometimes suffered heavily, in public favour and in influence, from the belief that it was too ardent in the pursuit of that policy; while at the same time it has always been in the worst odour with the Court of Rome, in consequence of its (I hope) unalterable attachment to Italian liberty and independence. I have sometimes been the spokesman of that party in recommendations which have tended to foster in fact the imputation I have mentioned, though not to warrant it as matter of reason. But it has existed in fact. So that while (as I think) general justice to society required that these things which I have now set forth should be written, special justice, as towards the party to which I am loyally attached, and which

* From 1847 to 1865 I sat for the University of Oxford.

I may have had a share in thus placing at a disadvantage before our countrymen, made it, to say the least, becoming that I should not shrink from writing them.

In discharging that office, I have sought to perform the part not of a theological partisan, but simply of a good citizen ; of one hopeful that many of his Roman Catholic friends and fellow-countrymen, who are, to say the least of it, as good citizens as himself, may perceive that the case is not a frivolous case, but one that merits their attention.

I will next proceed to give the reason why, up to a recent date, I have thought it right in the main to leave to any others, who might feel it, the duty of dealing in detail with this question.

The great change, which seems to me to have been brought about in the position of Roman Catholic Christians as citizens, reached its consummation, and came into full operation in July 1870, by the proceedings or so-called decrees of the Vatican Council.

Up to that time, opinion in the Roman Church on all matters involving civil liberty, though partially and sometimes widely intimidated, was free wherever it was resolute.   During the Middle Ages, heresy was often extinguished in blood, but in every Cisalpine country a principle of liberty, to a great extent, held its own, and national life refused to be put down. Nay more, these precious and inestimable gifts had not infrequently for their champions a local prelacy and clergy.   The Constitutions of Clarendon, cursed

from the Papal throne, were the work of the English
Bishops.   Stephen   Langton, [appointed   directly,
through an extraordinary stretch of power, by
Innocent III., to the See of Canterbury, headed the
Barons of England in extorting from the Papal
minion John, the worst and basest of all our
Sovereigns, that Magna Charta, which the Pope
at once visited with his anathemas.   In the reign
of Henry VIII., it was Tunstal, Bishop of Durham,
who first wrote against the Papal domination.
Tunstal was followed by Gardiner; and even the
recognition of the Royal Headship was voted by
the clergy, not under Cranmer, but under his unsus-
pected predecessor Warham.   Strong and domineer-
ing as was the high Papal party in those centuries,
the resistance was manful.   Thrice in history, it
seemed as if what we may call the Constitutional
party in the Church was about to triumph : first, at
the epoch of the Council of Constance; secondly,
when the French Episcopate was in conflict with
Pope Innocent XI.; thirdly, when Clement XIV.
levelled with the dust the deadliest foes that mental
and moral liberty have ever known.   But from July
1870, this state of things has passed away, and the
death-warrant of that Constitutional party has been
signed, and sealed, and promulgated in form.

Before that time arrived, although I had used expressions sufficiently indicative as to the tendency of
things in the great Latin Communion, yet I had for

very many years felt it to be the first and para-
mount duty of the British Legislature, whatever
Rome might say or do, to give to Ireland all that
justice could demand, in regard to matters of conscience and of civil equality, and thus to set herself
right in the opinion of the civilised world. So far
from seeing, what some believed they saw, a spirit of
unworthy compliance in such a course, it appeared
to me the only one which suited either the dignity
or the duty of my country. While this debt remained
unpaid, both before and after 1870, I did not think
it my province to open formally a line of argument
on a question of prospective rather than immediate
moment, which might have prejudiced the matter of
duty lying nearest our hand, and morally injured
Great Britain not less than Ireland, Churchmen and
Nonconformists not less than adherents of the Papal
Communion, by slackening the disposition to pay the
debt of justice. When Parliament had passed the
Church Act of 1869 and the Land Act of 1870, there
remained only, under the great head of Imperial
equity, one serious question to be dealt with—that of
the higher Education. I consider that the Liberal majority in the House of Commons, and the Government
to which I had the honour and satisfaction to belong,
formally tendered payment in full of this portion of
the debt by the Irish University Bill of February
1873. Some indeed think, that it was overpaid: a
question into which this is manifestly not place to

enter. But the Roman Catholic prelacy of Ireland thought fit to procure the rejection of that measure, by the direct influence which they exercised over a certain number of Irish Members of Parliament, and by the temptation which they thus offered—the bid, in effect, which (to use a homely phrase) they made, to attract the support of the Tory Opposition. Their efforts were crowned with a complete success. From that time forward I have felt that the situation was changed, and that important matters would have to be cleared by suitable explanations. The debt to Ireland had been paid : a debt to the country at large had still to be disposed of, and this has come to be the duty of the hour. So long, indeed, as I continued to be Prime Minister, I should not have considered a broad political discussion on a general question suitable to proceed from me ; while neither I nor (I am certain) my colleagues would have been disposed to run the risk of stirring popular passions by a vulgar and unexplained appeal. But every difficulty, arising from the necessary limitations of an official position, has now been removed.

VII. On the Home Policy of the Future.

I could not, however, conclude these observations without anticipating and answering an inquiry they suggest. "Are they, then," it will be asked, "a recantation and a regret ; and what are they meant to recommend as the policy of the future?" My reply shall be succinct and plain. Of what the Liberal party has accomplished, by word or deed, in establishing the full civil equality of Roman Catholics, I regret nothing, and I recant nothing.

It is certainly a political misfortune that, during the last thirty years, a Church so tainted in its views of civil obedience, and so unduly capable of changing its front and language after Emancipation from what it had been before, like an actor who has to perform several characters in one piece, should have acquired an extension of its hold upon the highest classes of this country. The conquests have been chiefly, as might have been expected, among women; but the number of male converts, or captives (as I might prefer to call them), has not been inconsiderable. There is no doubt, that every one of these secessions is in the nature of a considerable moral and social severance. The breadth of this gap varies, according to varieties of individual character. But it is too commonly a wide one. Too commonly, the spirit of the neophyte is expressed by the words which have become notorious : "a Catholic first, an Englishman afterwards." Words which properly convey no more than a truism; for every Christian must seek to place his religion even before his country in his inner heart. But very far from a truism in the sense in which we have been led to construe them. We take them to mean that the "convert" intends, in case of any conflict between the Queen and the Pope, to follow the Pope, and let the Queen shift for herself; which, happily, she can well do.

Usually, in this country, a movement in the highest class would raise a presumption of a similar movement in the mass. It is not so here. Rumours have gone about that the proportion of members of the Papal Church to the population has increased, especially in England. But these rumours would seem to be confuted by authentic figures. The Roman Catholic Marriages, which supply a competent test, and which were 4·89 per cent. of the whole in 1854, and 4·62 per cent. in 1859, were 4·09 per cent. in 1869, and 4·02 per cent. in 1871.

There is something at the least abnormal in such a partial growth, taking effect as it does among the wealthy and noble, while the people cannot be charmed, by any incantation, into the Roman camp. The original Gospel was supposed to be meant especially for the poor; but the gospel of the nineteenth century from Rome courts another and less modest destination. If the Pope does not control more souls among us, he certainly controls more acres.

The severance, however, of a certain number of lords of the soil from those who till it, can be borne. And so I trust will in like manner be endured the new and very real " aggression " of the principles promulgated by Papal authority, whether they are or are not loyally disclaimed. In this matter, each man is his own judge and his own guide : I can speak for myself. I am no longer able to say, as I would have said before 1870, "There is nothing in the necessary belief of the Roman Catholic which can appear to impeach his full civil title; for, whatsoever be the follies of ecclesiastical power in his Church, his Church itself has not required of him, with binding authority, to assent to any principles inconsistent with his civil duty." That ground is now, for the present at least, cut from under my feet. What then is to be our course of policy hereafter? First let me say that, as regards the great Imperial settlement, achieved by slow degrees, which has admitted men of all creeds subsisting among us to Parliament, that I conceive to be so determined beyond all doubt or question, as to have become one of the deep foundation-stones of the existing Constitution. But inasmuch as, short of this great charter of public liberty, and independently of all that has been done, there are pending matters of comparatively minor moment which have been, or may be, subjects of discussion, not without interest attaching to them, I can suppose a question to arise in the minds of some. My own views and intentions in the future are of the smallest significance. But, if the arguments I have here offered make it my duty to declare them, I say at once the future will be exactly as the past : in the little that depends on me, I shall be guided hereafter, as heretofore, by the rule of maintaining equal civil rights irrespectively of religious differences; and shall resist all attempts to exclude the members of the Roman Church from the benefit of that rule. Indeed I may say that I have already given conclusive indications of this view, by supporting in Parliament, as a Minister, since 1870, the repeal of the Ecclesiastical Titles Act, for what I think ample reasons. Not only because the time has not yet come when we can assume the consequences of the revolutionary measures of 1870 to have been thoroughly weighed and digested by all capable men in the Roman Communion. Not only because so great a numerical proportion are, as I have before observed, necessarily incapable of mastering, and forming their personal judgment upon, the case. Quite irrespectively even of these considerations, I hold that our onward even course should not be changed by follies, the consequences of which, if the worst come to the worst, this country will have alike the power and, in case of need, the will to control. The State will, I trust, be ever careful to leave the domain of religious conscience free, and yet to keep it to its own domain; and to allow neither private caprice nor, above all, foreign arrogance to dictate to it in the discharge of its proper office. "England expects every man to do his duty;" and none can be so well prepared under all circumstances to exact its performance as that Liberal party, which has done the work of justice alike for Nonconformists and for Papal dissidents, and whose members have so often, for the sake of that work, hazarded their credit with the markedly Protestant constituencies of the country. Strong the State of the United Kingdom has always been in material strength; and its moral panoply is now, we may hope, pretty complete.

It is not then for the dignity of the Crown and people of the United Kingdom to be diverted from a path which they have deliberately chosen, and which it does not rest with all the myrmidons of the Apostolic Chamber either openly to obstruct, or secretly to undermine.   It is rightfully to be expected, it is greatly to be desired, that the Roman Catholics of this country should do in the Nineteenth century what their forefathers of England, except a handful of emissaries, did in the Sixteenth, when they were marshalled in resistance to the Armada, and in the Seventeenth when, in despite of the Papal Chair, they sat in the House of Lords under the Oath of Allegiance.   That which we are entitled to desire, we are entitled also to expect : indeed, to say we did not expect it, would, in my judgment, be the true way of conveying an " insult " to those concerned.   In this expectation we may be partially disappointed.   Should those to whom I appeal, thus unhappily come to bear witness in their own persons to the decay of sound, manly, true life in their Church, it will be their loss more than ours. The inhabitants of these Islands, as a whole, are

F

stable, though sometimes credulous and excitable;
resolute, though sometimes boastful: and a strong-
headed and soundhearted race will not be hindered,
either by latent or by avowed dissents, due to the
foreign influence of a caste, from the accomplish-
ment of its mission in the world.

APPENDICES.

APPENDIX A.

The numbers here given correspond with those of the Eighteen Propositions given in the text, where it would have been less convenient to cite the originals.

1, 2, 3. " Ex quâ omnino falsâ socialis regiminis ideâ haud timent erroneam illam fovere opinionem, Catholicæ Ecclesiæ, animarumque saluti maxime exitialem, a rec. mem. Gregorio XIV. prædecessore Nostro *deliramentum* appellatam (eâdem Encycl. 'Mirari'), nimirum, libertatem conscientiæ et cultuum esse proprium cujuscunque hominis jus, quod lege proclamari, et asseri debet in omni recte constitutâ societate, et jus civibus inesse ad omnimodam libertatem nullâ vel ecclesiasticâ, vel civili auctoritate coarctandam, quo suos conceptus quoscumque sive voce sive typis, sive aliâ ratione palam publiceque manifestare ac declarare valeant."—*Encyclical Letter.*

4. " Atque silentio præterire non possumus eorum audaciam, qui sanam non sustinentes doctrinam ' illis Apostolicæ Sedis judiciis, et decretis, quorum objectum ad bonum generale Ecclesiæ, ejusdemque jura, ac disciplinam spectare declaratur, dummodo fidei morumque dogmata non attingat, posse assensum et obedientiam detrectari absque peccato, et absque ullâ Catholicæ professionis jacturâ.'"—*Ibid.*

5. " Ecclesia non est vera perfectaque societas plane libera, nec pollet suis propriis et constantibus juribus sibi a divino

suo Fundatore collatis, sed civilis potestatis est definire quæ
sint Ecclesiæ jura, ac limites, intra quos eadem jura exercere
queat."—*Syllabus* v.

6. "Romani Pontifices et Concilia œcumenica a limiti-
bus suæ potestatis recesserunt, jura Principum usurpârunt,
atque etiam in rebus fidei et morum definiendis errârunt."—
Ibid. xxiii.

7. "Ecclesia vis inferendæ potestatem non habet, neque
potestatem ullam temporalem directam vel indirectam."—
Ibid. xxiv.

8. "Præter potestatem episcopatui inhærentem, alia est
attributa temporalis potestas a civili imperio vel expressè vel
tacitè concessa, revocanda propterea, cum libuerit, a civili
imperio."—*Ibid.* xxv.

9. "Ecclesiæ et personarum ecclesiasticarum immunitas a
jure civili ortum habuit."—*Ibid.* xxx.

10. "In conflictu legum utriusque potestatis, jus civile
prævalet."—*Ibid.* xlii.

11. "Catholicis viris probari potest ea juventutis insti-
tuendæ ratio, quæ sit a Catholicâ fide et ab Ecclesiæ potestate
sejuncta, quæque rerum dumtaxat, naturalium scientiam ac
terrenæ socialis vitæ fines tantummodo vel saltem primarium
spectet."—*Ibid.* xlviii.

12. "Philosophicarum rerum morumque scientia, itemque
civiles leges possunt et debent a divinâ et ecclesiasticâ auctoritate declinare."—*Ibid.* lvii.

13. "Matrimonii sacramentum non est nisi contractui acces-
sorium ab eoque separabile, ipsumque sacramentum in unâ
tantum nuptiali benedictione situm est."—*Ibid.* lxvi.

"Vi contractûs mere civilis potest, inter Christianos con-
stare veri nominis matrimonium; falsumque est, aut contractum matrimonii inter Christianos semper esse sacramentum,
aut nullum esse contractum, si sacramentum excludatur."
—*Ibid.* lxxiii.

14. "De temporalis regni cum spirituali compatibilitate

disputant inter se Christianæ et Catholicæ Ecclesiæ filii."—
Syllabus lxxv.

15. "Abrogatio civilis imperii, quo Apostolica Sedes poti-
tur, ad Ecclesiæ libertatem felicitatemque vel maxime con-
duceret."—*Ibid.* lxxvi.

16. "Ætate hac nostra non amplius expedit religionem
Catholicam haberi tanquam unicam status religionem, cæteris
quibuscumque cultibus exclusis."—*Ibid.* lxxvii.

17. "Hinc laudabiliter in quibusdam Catholici nominis
regionibus lege cautum est, ut hominibus illuc immigrantibus
liceat publicum proprii cujusque cultus exercitium habere."
—*Ibid.* lxxviii.

18. "Romanus Pontifex potest ac debet cum progressu,
cum liberalismo et cum recenti civilitate sese reconciliare et
componere."—*Ibid.* lxxx.

APPENDIX B.

I have contented myself with a minimum of citation from
the documents of the period before Emancipation. Their full
effect can only be gathered by such as are acquainted with,
or will take the trouble to refer largely to the originals. It
is worth while, however, to cite the following passage from
Bishop Doyle, as it may convey, through the indignation it
expresses, an idea of the amplitude of the assurances which
had been (as I believe, most honestly and sincerely) given.

"There is no justice, my Lord, in thus condemning us.
Such conduct on the part of our opponents creates in our
bosoms a sense of wrong being done to us; it exhausts our
patience, it provokes our indignation, and prevents us from
reiterating our efforts to obtain a more impartial hearing.
We are tempted, in such cases as these, to attribute unfair
motives to those who differ from us, as we cannot conceive

how men gifted with intelligence can fail to discover truths
so plainly demonstrated as,

 " That our faith or our allegiance is not regulated by any
such doctrines as those imputed to us;

 " That our duties to the Government of our country are
not influenced nor affected by any Bulls or practices of
Popes;

 " That these duties are to be learned by us, as by every
other class of His Majesty's subjects, from the Gospel, from
the reason given to us by God, from that love of country
which nature has implanted in our hearts, and from those
constitutional maxims, which are as well understood, and as
highly appreciated, by Catholics of the present day, as by
their ancestors, who founded them with Alfred, or secured
them at Runnymede."—*Doyle's ' Essay on the Catholic Claims,'*
London, 1826, p. 38.

 The same general tone, as in 1826, was maintained in the
answers of the witnesses from Maynooth College before the
Commission of 1855. See, for example, pp. 132, 161–4,
272–3, 275, 361, 370–5, 381–2, 394–6, 405. The Commission
reported (p. 64), " We see no reason to believe that there
has been any disloyalty in the teaching of the College, or
any disposition to impair the obligations of an unreserved
allegiance to your Majesty.'

APPENDIX C.

 Compare the recent and ominous forecasting of the future
European policy of the British Crown, in an Article from a
Romish Periodical for the current month, which has direct
relation to these matters, and which has every appearance of
proceeding from authority.

 " Surely in any European complication, such as may any
day arise, nay, such as must ere long arise, from the natural

gravitation of the forces, which are for the moment kept in check and truce by the necessity of preparation for their inevitable collision, it may very well be that the future prosperity of England may be staked in the struggle, and that the side which she may take may be determined, not either by justice or interest, but *by a passionate resolve to keep up the Italian kingdom at any hazard.*"—The ' *Month* ' for November, 1874: ' Mr. Gladstone's Durham Letter,' p. 265.

This is a remarkable disclosure. With *whom* could England be brought into conflict by any disposition she might feel to keep up the Italian kingdom? Considered as States, both Austria and France are in complete harmony with Italy. But it is plain that Italy has some enemy; and the writers of the ' Month ' appear to know who it is.

APPENDIX D.

Notice has been taken, both in this country and abroad, of the apparent inertness of public men, and of at least one British Administration, with respect to the subject of these pages. See Friedberg, ' Gränzen zwischen Staat und Kirche,' Abtheilung iii. pp. 755–6; and the Preface to the Fifth Volume of Mr. Greenwood's elaborate, able, and judicial work, entitled ' Cathedra Petri,' p. iv.

" If there be any chance of such a revival, it would become our political leaders to look more closely into the peculiarities of a system, which denies the right of the subject to freedom of thought and action upon matters most material to his civil and religious welfare. There is no mode of ascertaining the spirit and tendency of great institutions but in a careful study of their history. The writer is profoundly impressed with the conviction that our political instructors have wholly neglected this important duty: or, which is perhaps worse, left it in the hands of a class of persons whose zeal has outrun their discretion, and who have sought rather to engage the prejudices than the judgment of their hearers in the cause they have, no doubt sincerely, at heart."

LONDON: PRINTED BY WILLIAM CLOWES AND SONS, STAMFORD STREET
AND CHARING CROSS.

A LETTER

ADDRESSED TO HIS GRACE

THE DUKE OF NORFOLK

ON OCCASION OF

MR. GLADSTONE'S RECENT EXPOSTULATION

BY

JOHN HENRY NEWMAN D.D.

OF THE ORATORY

LONDON

B M PICKERING 196 PICCADILLY

1875

LONDON :

S. AND J. BRAWN, PRINTERS, PRINCES STREET, LITTLE QUEEN STREET,

HIGH HOLBORN, W.C.

TO HIS GRACE THE DUKE OF NORFOLK,

HEREDITARY EARL MARSHAL OF ENGLAND,

&c., &c.

MY DEAR DUKE OF NORFOLK,

When I yielded to the earnest wish which you,
together with many others, urged upon me, that I should
reply to Mr. Gladstone's recent Expostulation, a friend
suggested that I ought to ask your Grace's permission to
address my remarks to you. Not that for a moment he
or I thought of implicating you, in any sense or measure,
in a responsibility which is solely and entirely my own;
but on a very serious occasion, when such heavy charges
had been made against the Catholics of England by so
powerful and so earnest an adversary, it seemed my duty,
in meeting his challenge, to gain the support, if I could,
of a name, which is the special representative and the
fitting sample of a laity, as zealous for the Catholic Religion
as it is patriotic.

You consented with something of the reluctance which
I had felt myself when called upon to write; for it was
hard to be summoned at any age, early or late, from a
peaceful course of life and the duties of one's station, to a
scene of war. Still, you consented; and for myself, it is
the compensation for a very unpleasant task, that I, who
belong to a generation that is fast flitting away, am thus
enabled, in what is likely to be my last publication, to associate myself with one, on many accounts so dear to me,—so
full of young promise—whose career is before him.

I deeply grieve that Mr. Gladstone has felt it his duty to speak with such extraordinary severity of our Religion and of ourselves. I consider he has committed himself to a representation of ecclesiastical documents which will not hold, and to a view of our position in the country which we have neither deserved nor can be patient under. None but the *Schola Theologorum* is competent to determine the force of Pàpal and Synodal utterances, and the exact interpretation of them is a work of time. But so much may be safely said of the decrees which have lately been promulgated, and of the faithful who have received them, that Mr. Gladstone's account, both of them and of us, is neither trustworthy nor charitable.

Yet not a little may be said in explanation of a step, which so many of his admirers and well-wishers deplore. I own to a deep feeling, that Catholics may in good measure thank themselves, and no one else, for having alienated from them so religious a mind. There are those among us, as it must be confessed, who for years past have conducted themselves as if no responsibility attached to wild words and overbearing deeds; who have stated truths in the most paradoxical form, and stretched principles till they were close upon snapping; and who at length, having done their best to set the house on fire, leave to others the task of putting out the flame. The English people are sufficiently sensitive of the claims of the Pope, without having them, as if in defiance, flourished in their faces. Those claims most certainly I am not going to deny; I have never denied them. I have no intention, now that I have to write upon them, to conceal any part of them. And I uphold them as heartily as I recognize my duty of loyalty to the constitution, the laws, and the government of England. I see no inconsistency in my being at once a good Catholic and a good Englishman. Yet it is one thing to be able to satisfy myself as to my consistency, quite another to satisfy others; and, undisturbed as I am in my own conscience, I have great difficulties in the task before me. I have one difficulty to overcome in the present excitement of the public mind against our Religion, caused partly by the chronic extravagances of knots of Catholics here and there, partly by the vehement rhetoric which is the occasion of my writing to you. A worse difficulty lies in getting people, as they are commonly found, to put off the modes of speech and language which are usual with them, and to enter into scientific distinctions and traditionary rules of interpretation, which, as being new to them, appear evasive and unnatural. And a third difficulty, as I may call it, is this—that in so very wide a subject, opening so great a variety of questions, and of opinions upon them, while it will be simply necessary to take the objections made against us and our faith, one by one, readers may think me trifling with their patience, because they do not find those points first dealt with, on which they lay most stress themselves.

But I have said enough by way of preface; and without more delay turn to Mr. Gladstone's pamphlet.

§ 1. Introductory Remarks.

The main question which Mr. Gladstone has started I consider to be this :—Can Catholics be trustworthy subjects of the State ? has not a foreign Power a hold over their consciences such, that it may at any time be used to the serious perplexity and injury of the civil government under which they live ? Not that Mr. Gladstone confines himself to these questions, for he goes out of his way, I am sorry to say, to taunt us with our loss of mental and moral freedom, a vituperation which is not necessary for his purpose at all. He informs us too that we have "repudiated ancient history," and are rejecting "modern thought," and that our Church has been "refurbishing her rusty tools," and has been lately aggravating, and is likely still more to aggravate, our state of bondage. I think it unworthy of Mr. Gladstone's high character thus to have inveighed against us ; what intellectual manliness is left to us, according to him ? yet his circle of acquaintance is too wide, and his knowledge of his countrymen on the other hand too accurate, for him not to know that he is bringing a great amount of odium and bad feeling upon excellent men, whose only offence is their religion. The more intense is the prejudice with which we are regarded by whole classes of men, the less is there of generosity in his pouring upon us superfluous reproaches. The graver the charge, which is the direct occasion of his writing against us, the more careful should he be not to prejudice judge and jury to our disadvantage. No rhetoric is needed in England against an unfortunate Catholic at any time ; but so little is Mr. Gladstone conscious of his treatment of us that in one place of his Pamphlet, strange as it may seem, he makes it his boast that he has been careful to " do nothing towards importing passion into what is matter of pure argument" pp. 15, 16. I venture to think he will one day be sorry for what he has said.

However, we must take things as we find them ; and what I propose to do is this—to put aside, unless it comes directly in my way, his accusation against us of repudiating ancient history, rejecting modern thought, and renouncing our mental freedom, and to confine myself for the most part to what he principally insists upon, that Catholics, if they act consistently with their principles, cannot be loyal subjects ;—I shall not, however, omit notice of his attack upon our moral uprightness.

The occasion and the grounds of Mr. Gladstone's impeachment of us, if I understand him, are as follows :—He was alarmed, as a statesman, ten years ago by the Pope's Encyclical of December 8, and by the Syllabus of Erroneous Propositions which, by the Pope's authority, accompanied its transmission to the bishops. Then came the Definitions of the Vatican Council in 1870, upon the universal jurisdiction and doctrinal infallibility of the Pope. And lastly, as the event which turned alarm into indignation, and into the duty of public remonstrance, "the Roman Catholic Prelacy of Ireland thought fit to procure the rejection of" the Irish University Bill of February, 1873, "by the direct influence which they exercised over a certain number of Irish Members of Parliament, &c." p. 60. This step on the part of the bishops showed, if I understand him, the new and mischievous force which had been acquired at Rome by the late acts there, or at least left him at liberty, by causing his loss of power, to denounce it. "From that time forward the situation was changed," and an opening was made for a "broad political discussion" on the subject of the Catholic religion and its professors, and "a debt to the country had to be disposed of." That debt, if I am right, will be paid, if he can ascertain, on behalf of the country, that there is nothing in the Catholic Religion to hinder its professors from being as loyal as other subjects of the State, and that the See of Rome cannot interfere with their civil duties so as to give the civil power trouble or alarm. The main ground on which he relies for the necessity of some such inquiry is, first, the text of the authoritative documents of 1864 and 1870 ;

next, and still more, the *animus* which they breathe, and the sustained aggressive spirit which they disclose ; and, thirdly, the daring deed of aggression in 1873, when the Pope, acting (as it is alleged) upon the Irish Members of Parliament, succeeded in ousting from their seats a ministry who, besides past benefits, were at that very time doing for Irish Catholics, and therefore ousted for doing, a special service.

Now, it would be preposterous and officious in me to put myelf forwa rd as champion for the Venerable Prelacy of Ireland, or to take upon myself the part of advocate and representative of the Holy See. "Non tali auxilio ;" in neither character could I come forward without great presumption ; not the least for this reason, because I cannot know the exact points which are really the *gist* of the affront, which Mr. Gladstone conceives he has sustained, whether from the one quarter or from the other ; yet in a question so nearly interesting myself as that February bill, which he brought into the House, in great sincerity and kindness, for the benefit of the Catholic University in Ireland, I may be allowed to say thus much—that I, who now have no official relation to the Irish Bishops, and am not in any sense in the counsels of Rome, felt at once, when I first saw the outline of that bill, the greatest astonishment on reading one of its provisions, and a dread which painfully affected me, lest Mr. Gladstone perhaps was acting on an understanding with the Catholic Prelacy. I did not see how in honour they could accept it. It was possible, did the question come over again, to decide in favour of the Queen's Colleges, and to leave the project of a Catholic University alone. The Holy See might so have decided in 1847. But at or about that date, three re-scripts had come from Rome in favour of a distinctively Catholic Institution ; a National Council had decided in its favour ; large offers of the Government had been rejected ; great commotions had been caused in the political world, munificent contributions had been made, all on the sole principle that Catholic teaching was to be upheld in the country inviolate, If, then, for the sake of a money grant, or other secular advantage, this ground of principle was deserted, and

Catholic youths after all were allowed to attend the lectures of men of no religion, or of the Protestant, the contest of thirty years would have been stultified, and the Pope and the Bishops would seem to have been playing a game, while putting forward the plea of conscience and religious duty. I hoped that the clause in the Bill, which gave me such uneasiness, could have been omitted from it; but, any how, it was an extreme relief to me when the papers announced that the Bishops had expressed their formal dissatisfaction with it.

They determined to decline a gift laden with such a condition, and who can blame them for so doing? who can be surprised that they should now do what they did in 1847? what new move in politics was it, if they so determined? what was there in it of a factious character? Is the Catholic Irish interest the only one which is not to be represented in the House of Commons? Why is not that interest as much a matter of right as any other? I fear to expose my own ignorance of Parliamentary rules and proceedings, but I had supposed that the railway interest, and what is called the publican interest, were very powerful there : in Scotland, too, I believe, a government has a formidable party to deal with; and, to revert to Ireland, there are the Home-rulers, who have objects in view quite distinct from, or contrary to, those of the Catholic hierarchy. As to the Pope, looking at the surface of things, there is nothing to suggest that he interfered, there was no necessity of interference, on so plain a point; and, when an act can be sufficiently accounted for without introducing an hypothetical cause, it is bad logic to introduce it. Speaking according to my lights, I altogether disbelieve the interposition of Rome in the matter. In the proceedings which they adopted, the Bishops were only using civil rights, common to all, which others also used and in their own way. Why might it not be their duty to promote the interests of their religion by means of their political opportunities? Is there no Exeter Hall interest? I thought it was a received theory of our Reformed Constitution that Members of Parliament were representatives, and in some sort delegates of their constituents, and that the strength of each interest was shown, and the course of the nation determined, by the divisions in the House of Commons. I recollect the " Times " intimating its regret, after one general election, that there was no English Catholic in the new House, on the ground that every class and party should be represented there. Surely the Catholic religion has not a small party in Ireland ; why then should it not have a corresponding number of exponents and defenders at Westminster? So clear does this seem to me, that I think there must be some defect in my knowledge of facts to explain Mr. Gladstone's surprise and displeasure at the conduct of the Irish Prelacy in 1873 ; yet I suspect none ; and, if there be none, then his unreasonableness in this instance of Ireland makes it not unlikely that he is unreasonable also in his judgment of the Encyclical, Syllabus, and Vatican Decrees.

However, the Bishops, I believe, not only opposed Mr. Gladstone's bill, but, instead of it, they asked for some money grant towards the expenses of their University. If so, their obvious argument was this—that Catholics formed the great majority of the population of Ireland, and it was not fair that the Protestant minority should have all that was bestowed in endowment or otherwise upon Education. To this the reply, I suppose, would be, that it was not Protestantism, but liberal education that had the money, and that, if the Bishops chose to give up their own principles and act as Liberals, they might have the benefit of it too. I am not concerned here with these arguments, but I wish to notice the position which the Bishops would occupy in urging such a request :—I must not say that they were Irishmen first and Catholics afterwards, but I do say that in such a demand they spoke not simply as Catholic Bishops, but as the Bishops of a Catholic nation. They did not speak from any promptings of the Encyclical, Syllabus, or Vatican Decrees. They claimed as Irishmen a share in the endowments of the country ; and has not Ireland surely a right to speak in such a matter, and might not her Bishops fairly represent her? It seems to me a great mistake to think that every thing that is done by the Irish Bishops and clergy is done on an ecclesiastical motive ; why not on a national ? but if so, such acts have nothing to do with Rome. I know well what simple firm faith the great body of the Irish people have, and how they put the Catholic Religion before anything else in the world. It is their comfort, their joy, their treasure, their boast, their compensation for a hundred worldly disadvantages ; but who can deny that in politics their conduct at times—nay, more than at times—has had a flavour rather of their nation than of their Church ? Only in the last general election this was said, when they were so earnest for Home Rule. Why, then, must Mr. Gladstone come down upon the Catholic Religion, because the Irish love dearly the Green Island, and its interests ? Ireland is not the only country in which politics, or patriotism, or party, has been so closely associated with religion in the nation or a class, that it is difficult to say which of the various motive principles was uppermost. "The Puritan," says Macaulay, "prostrated himself in the dust before his Maker, but he set his foot on the neck of his king :" I am not accusing such a man of hypocrisy on account of this ; having great wrongs, as he considered, both in religious and temporal matters, and the authors of these distinct wrongs being the same persons, he did not nicely discriminate between the acts which he did as a patriot and the acts which he did as a Puritan. And so as regards Irishmen, they do not, cannot, distinguish between their love of Ireland and their love of religion ; their patriotism is religious, and their religion is strongly tinctured with patriotism ; and it is hard to recognize the abstract and ideal Ultramontane, pure and simple, in the concrete exhibition of him in flesh and blood as found in the polling booth or in his chapel. I do not see how the Pope can be made answerable for him in any of his political acts during the last fifty years.

This leads me to a subject, of which Mr. Gladstone makes a good deal in his Pamphlet. I will say of a great man, whom he quotes, and for whose memory I have a great respect, I mean Bishop Doyle, that there was just a little tinge of patriotism in the way in which, on one occasion, he speaks of the Pope. I dare say any of us would have done the same, in the heat of a great struggle for national liberty, for he said nothing but what was true and honest ; I only mean that the energetic language which he used was not exactly such as would have suited the atmosphere of Rome.   He says to Lord Liverpool, " We are taunted with the proceedings of Popes. What, my Lord, have we Catholics to do with the proceedings of Popes, or why should we be made accountable for them ?" p. 27. Now, with some proceedings of Popes, we Catholics have very much to do indeed ; but, if the context of his words is consulted, I make no doubt it will be found that he was referring to certain proceedings of certain Popes, when he said that Catholics had no part of their responsibility.   Assuredly there are certain acts of Popes in which no one would like to have part. Then, again, his words require some pious interpretation when he says that " the allegiance due to the king and the allegiance due to the Pope, are as distinct and as divided in their nature as any two things can possibly be," p. 30. Yes, in their nature, in the abstract, but not in the particular case ; for a heathen State might bid me throw incense upon the altar of Jupiter, and the Pope would bid me not to do so.   I venture to make the same remark on the Address of the Irish Bishops to their clergy and laity, quoted at p. 31, and on the Declaration of the Vicars Apostolic in England, *ibid.*

But I must not be supposed for an instant to mean, in what I have said, that the venerable men, to whom I have referred, were aware of any ambiguity either in such statements as the above, or in others which were denials of the Pope's infallibility. Indeed, one of them at an earlier date, 1793, Dr. Troy, Archbishop of Dublin, had introduced into one of his Pastorals the subject, which Mr. Gladstone considers they so summarily disposed of. The Archbishop says :—" Many Catholics contend that the Pope, when teaching the universal Church, as their supreme visible head and pastor, as successor to St. Peter, and heir to the promises of special assistance made to him by Jesus Christ, is infallible ; and that his decrees and decisions in that capacity are to be respected as rules of faith, when they are dogmatical or confined to doctrinal points of faith and morals. Others deny this, and require the expressed or tacit acquiescence of the Church, assembled or dispersed, to stamp infallibility on his dogmatical decrees. Until the Church shall decide upon this question of the Schools, either opinion may be adopted by individual Catholics, without any breach of Catholic communion or peace. The Catholics of Ireland have lately declared, that it is not an article of the Catholic faith; nor are they thereby required to believe or profess that the Pope is infallible, without adopting or abjuring either of the recited opinions which are open to discussion, while the Church continues silent about them." The Archbishop thus addressed his flock, at the time when he was informing them that the Pope had altered the oath which was taken by the Catholic Bishops.

As to the language of the Bishops in 1826, we must recollect that at that time the clergy, both of Ireland and England, were educated in Gallican opinions. They took those opinions for granted, and they thought, if they went so far as to ask themselves the question, that the definition of Papal Infallibility was simply impossible. Even among those at the Vatican Council, who themselves personally believed in it, I believe there were Bishops who, until the actual definition had been passed, thought that such a definition could not be made. Perhaps they would argue that, though the historical evidence was sufficient for their own personal conviction, it was not sufficiently clear of difficulties to make it safe to impose it on Catholics as a dogma. Much more would this be the feeling of the Bishops in 1826. "How," they would ask, "can it ever come to pass that a majority of our order should find it their duty to relinquish their prime prerogative, and to make the Church take the shape of a pure monarchy?" They would think its definition as much out of the question, as that, in twenty-five years after their time, there would be a hierarchy of thirteen Bishops in England, with a Cardinal for Archbishop.

But, all this while, such modes of thinking were foreign altogether to the minds of the *entourage* of the Holy See. Mr. Gladstone himself says, and the Duke of Wellington and Sir Robert Peel must have known it as well as he, "The Popes have kept up, with comparatively little intermission, for well nigh a thousand years, their claim to dogmatic infallibility," p. 28. Then, if the Pope's claim to infallibility was so patent a fact, could they ever suppose that he could be brought to admit that it was hopeless to turn that claim into a dogma? In truth, those ministers were very little interested in that question; as was said in a Petition or Declaration, signed among others by Dr. Troy, it was "immaterial in a political light;" but, even if they thought it material, or if there were other questions they wanted to ask, why go to Bishop Doyle? If they wanted to obtain some real information about the probabilities of the future, why did they not go to head-quarters? Why did they potter about the halls of Universities in this matter of Papal exorbitances, or rely upon the pamphlets or examinations of Bishops whom they never asked for their credentials? Why not go at once to Rome?

The reason is plain: it was a most notable instance, with a grave consequence, of what is a fixed tradition with us the English people, and a great embarrassment to every administration in their dealings with Catholics. I recollect, years ago, Dr. Griffiths, Vicar Apostolic of the London District, giving me an account of an interview he had with the late Lord Derby, then I suppose Colonial Secretary. I understood him to say that Lord Derby was in perplexity at the time, on some West India matter, in which Catholics were concerned, because he could not find their responsible representative. He wanted Dr. Griffiths to undertake the office, and expressed something of disappointment when the Bishop felt obliged to decline it. A chronic malady has from time to time its paroxysms, and the history on which I am now engaged is a serious instance of it. I think it is impossible that the British government could have entered into formal negociations with the Pope, without its transpiring in the course of them, and its becoming perfectly clear, that Rome could never be a party to such a pledge as England wanted, and that no pledge from Catholics was of any value to which Rome was not a party.

But no ; they persisted in an enterprise which was hopeless in its first principle, for they thought to break the indissoluble tie which bound together the head and the members,—and doubtless Rome felt the insult, though she might think it prudent not to notice it. France was not the keystone of the ecumenical power, though her Church was so great and so famous ; nor could the hierarchy of Ireland, in spite of its fidelity to the Catholic faith, give any pledge of the future to the statesmen who required one ; there was but one See, whose word was worth anything in the matter, " that church " (to use the language of the earliest of our Doctors) " to which the faithful all round about are bound to have recourse." Yet for three hundred years it has been the official rule with England to ignore the existence of the Pope, and to deal with Catholics in England, not as his children, but as sectaries of the Roman Catholic persuasion. Napoleon said to his envoy, " Treat with the Pope as if he was master of 100,000 men." So clearly did he, from mere worldly sagacity, comprehend the Pope's place in the then state of European affairs, as to say that, " if the Pope had not existed, it would have been well to have created him for that occasion, as the Roman consuls created a dictator in difficult circumstances." (Alison's *Hist.* ch. 35). But we, in the instance of the greatest, the oldest power in Europe, a Church whose grandeur in past history demanded, one would think, some reverence in our treatment of her, the mother of English Christianity, who, whether her subsequent conduct had always been motherly or not, had been a true friend to us in the beginnings of our history, her we have not only renounced, but, to use a familiar word, we have absolutely cut. Time has gone on and we have no relentings ; to-day, as little as yesterday, do we understand that pride was not made for man, nor the cuddling of resentments for a great people. I am entering into no theological question : I am speaking all along of mere decent secular intercourse between England and Rome. A hundred grievances would have been set right on their first uprising, had there been a frank diplomatic understanding between two great powers ; but, on the contrary, even within the last few weeks, the present Ministry has destroyed any hope of a better state of things by withdrawing from the Vatican the make-shift channel of intercourse which had of late years been permitted there.

The world's politics has its laws; and such abnormal courses as England has pursued have their *Nemesis*. An event has taken place which, alas, already makes itself felt in issues, unfortunate for English Catholics certainly, but also, as I think, for our country. A great Council has been called; and, as England has for so long a time ignored Rome, Rome, I suppose, it must be said, has in turn ignored England. I do not mean of set purpose ignored, but as the natural consequence of our act. Bishops brought from the corners of the earth, in 1870, what could they know of English blue books and Parliamentary debates in the years 1826 and 1829? It was an extraordinary gathering, and its possibility, its purpose, and its issue, were alike marvellous, as depending on a coincidence of strange conditions, which, as might be said beforehand, never could take place. Such was the long reign of the Pope, in itself a marvel, as being the sole exception to a recognized ecclesiastical tradition. Only a Pontiff so unfortunate, so revered, so largely loved, so popular even with Protestants, with such a prestige of long sovereignty, with such claims on the Bishops around him, both of age and of paternal gracious acts, only such a man could have harmonized and guided to the conclusion, which he pointed out, an assembly so variously composed. And, considering the state of theological opinion seventy years before, not less marvellous was the concurrence of all but a few out of so many hundred Bishops in the theological judgment, so long desired at Rome; the protest made by some eighty or ninety, at the termination of the Council, against the proceedings of the vast majority lying, not against the truth of the doctrine then defined, but against its opportuneness. Nor less to be noted is the neglect of the Catholic powers to send representatives to the Council, who might have laid before the Fathers its political bearings. For myself, I did not call it inopportune, for times and seasons are known to God alone, and persecution may be as opportune, though not so pleasant as peace; nor, in accepting as a dogma what I had ever held as a truth, could I be doing violence to any theological view or conclusion of my own; nor has the acceptance of it any logical or practical effect whatever, as I consider, in weakening my allegiance to Queen Victoria; but there are few Catholics, I think, who will not deeply regret, though no one be in fault, that the English and Irish Prelacies of 1826, did not foresee the possibility of the Synodal determinations of 1870, nor will they wonder that Statesmen should feel themselves aggrieved, that stipulations, which they considered necessary for Catholic emancipation should have been, as they may think, rudely cast to the winds.

And now I must pass from the mere accidents of the controversy to its essential points, and I cannot treat them to the satisfaction of Mr. Gladstone, unless I go back a great way, and be allowed to speak of the ancient Catholic Church.

§ 2. The Ancient Church.

When Mr. Gladstone accuses us of " repudiating ancient history," he means the ancient history of the Church ; also, I understand him to be viewing that history under a particular aspect. There are many aspects in which Christianity presents itself to us ; for instance, the aspect of social usefulness, or of devotion, or again of theology ; but, though he in one place glances at the last of these aspects, his own view of it is its relation towards the civil power. He writes " as one of the world at large ;" as a "layman who has spent most and the best years of his life in the observation and practice of politics ;" p. 7, and, as a statesman, he naturally looks at the Church on its political side. Accordingly, in his title-page, in which he professes to be expostulating with us for accepting the Vatican Decrees, he does so, not for any reason whatever, but because of their incompatibility with our civil allegiance. This is the key-note of his impeachment of us. As a public man, he has only to do with the public action and effect of our Religion, its aspect upon national affairs, on our civil duties, on our foreign interests ; and he tells us that our Religion has a bearing and behaviour towards the State utterly unlike that of ancient Christianity, so unlike that we may be said to repudiate what Christianity was in its first centuries, so unlike to what it was then, that we have actually forfeited the proud boast of being "Ever one and the same ;" unlike, I say, in this, that our action is so antagonistic to the State's action, and our claims so menacing to civil peace and prosperity. Indeed! then I suppose our Lord and His Apostles, that St. Ignatius of Antioch, and St. Polycarp of Smyrna, and St. Cyprian of Carthage, and St. Laurence of Rome, that St. Alexander and St. Paul of Constantinople, that St. Ambrose of Milan, that Popes Leo, John, Sylverian, Gregory, and Martin, all members of the " undivided Church," cared supremely, and laboured successfully, to cultivate peaceful relations with the government of Rome. They had no doctrines and precepts, no rules of life, no isolation and aggressiveness, which caused them to be considered, in spite of themselves, the enemies of the human race! May I not, without disrespect, submit to Mr. Gladstone that this is very paradoxical? Surely it is our fidelity to the history of our forefathers, and not its repudiation, which Mr. Gladstone dislikes in us. When, indeed, was it in ancient times that the State did not show jealousy of the Church? Was it when Decius and Dioclesian slaughtered their thousands who had abjured the religion of old Rome? or, was it when Athanasius was banished to Treves? or when Basil, on the Imperial Prefect's crying out, "Never before did any man make so free with me," answered, "Perhaps you never before fell in with a Bishop?" or when Chrysostom was sent off to Cucusus, to be worried to death by an Empress? Go through the long annals of Church History, century after century, and say, was there ever a time when her Bishops, and notably the Bishop of Rome, were slow to give their testimony in behalf of the moral and revealed law and to suffer for their obedience to it, or forgot that they had a message to deliver to the world? not the task merely of administering spiritual consolation, or of making the sick-bed easy, or of training up good members of society, and of "serving tables," (though all this was included in their range of duty); but specially and directly to deliver a message to the world, a definite message to high and low, from the world's Maker, whether men would hear or whether they would forbear? The history surely of the Church in all past times, ancient as well as medieval, is the very embodiment of that tradition of Apostolical independence and freedom of speech which in the eyes of man is her great offence now.

Nay, that independence, I may say, is even one of her Notes or credentials; for where shall we find it except in the Catholic Church? "I spoke of Thy testimonies," says the Psalmist, "even before kings, and I was not ashamed." This verse, I think Dr. Arnold used to say, rose up in judgment against the Anglican Church, in spite of its real excellences.   As to the Oriental Churches, every one knows in what bondage they lie, whether they are under the rule of the Czar or of the Sultan.   Such is the actual fact that, whereas it is the very mission of Christianity to bear witness to the Creed and Ten Commandments in a world which is averse to them, Rome is now the one faithful representative, and thereby is heir and successor of that freespoken dauntless Church of old, whose traditions Mr. Gladstone says the said Rome has repudiated.

I have one thing more to say on the subject of the " semper eadem."   In truth, this fidelity to the ancient Christian system, seen in modern Rome, was the luminous fact which more than any other turned men's minds at Oxford forty years ago to look towards her with reverence, interest, and love.   It affected individual minds variously of course ; some it even brought on eventually to conversion, others it only restrained from active opposition to her claims ; but no one could read the Fathers, and determine to be their disciple, without feeling that Rome, like a faithful steward, had kept in fulness and in vigour what his own communion had let drop.   The Tracts for the Times were founded on a deadly antagonism to what in these last centuries has been called Erastianism or Cæsarism.   Their writers considered the Church to be a divine creation, " not of men, neither by man, but by Jesus Christ," the Ark of Salvation, the Oracle of Truth, the Bride of Christ, with a message to all men every where, and a claim on their love and obedience ; and, in relation to the civil power, the object of that promise of the Jewish prophets, " Behold, I will lift up My Hand to the Gentiles, and will set up My standard to the peoples, kings and their queens shall bow down to thee with their face toward the earth, and they shall lick up the dust of thy feet."   No Ultramontane (so called) could go beyond those writers in the account which they gave of her from the Prophets, and that high notion is recorded beyond mistake in a thousand passages of their writings.

There is a fine passage of Mr. Keble's in the British Critic, in animadversion upon a contemporary reviewer.   Mr.

Hurrell Froude, speaking of the Church of England, had said that "she was 'united' to the State as Israel to Egypt." This shocked the reviewer in question, who exclaimed in consequence, "The Church is *not* united to the State as Israel to Egypt; it is united as a believing *wife* to a *husband* who threatened to apostatize; and, as a Christian wife so placed would act . . clinging to the connection . . so the Church must struggle even now, and save, not herself, but the State,, from the crime of a *divorce*." On this Mr. Keble says, "We had thought that the Spouse of the Church was a very different Person from any or all States, and her relation to the State through Him *very unlike that of hers, whose duties are summed up in ' love, service, cherishing, and obedience.'* And since the one is exclusively of this world, the other essentially of the eternal world, *such an Alliance* as the above sentence describes, would have seemed to us, *not only fatal, but monstrous!*"* And he quotes the lines,—

" Mortua quinetiam jungebat corpora vivis,
 Componens manibusque manus, atque oribus ora :
 Tormenti genus ! "

It was this same conviction that the Church had rights which the State could not touch, and was prone to ignore, and which in consequence were the occasion of great troubles between the two, that led Mr. Froude at the beginning of the movement to translate the letters of St. Thomas Becket, and Mr. Bowden to write the Life of Hildebrand. As to myself, I will but refer, as to one out of many passages with the same drift, in the books and tracts which I published at that time, to my Whit-Monday and Whit-Tuesday Sermons.

I believe a large number of members of the Church of England at this time are faithful to the doctrine which was proclaimed within its pale in 1833, and following years ; the main difference between them and Catholics being, not as

---

* Review of Gladstone's " *The State in its Relations with the Church,*" October, 1839.

to the existence of certain high prerogatives and spiritual powers in the Christian Church, but that the powers which we give to the Holy See, they lodge in her Bishops and Priests, whether as a body or individually. Of course, this is a very important difference, but it does not enter into my argument here. It does seem to me preposterous to charge the Catholic Church of to-day with repudiating ancient history by certain political acts of hers, and thereby losing her identity, when it was her very likeness in political action to the Church of the first centuries, that has in our time attracted even to her communion, or at least to her teaching, not a few educated men, who made those first centuries their special model.

But I have more to say on this subject, perhaps too much, when I go on, as I now do, to contemplate the Christian Church, when persecution was exchanged for establishment, and her enemies became her children. As she resisted and defied her persecutors, so she ruled her convert people. And surely this was but natural, and will startle those only to whom the subject is new. If the Church is independent of the State, so far as she is a messenger from God, therefore, should the State, with its high officials and its subject masses, come into her communion, it is plain that they must at once change hostility into submission. There was no middle term ; either they must deny her claim to divinity or humble themselves before it,—that is, as far as the domain of religion extends, and that domain is a wide one. They could not place God and man on one level. We see this principle carried out among ourselves in all sects every day, though with greater or less exactness of application, according to the supernatural power which they ascribe to their ministers or clergy. It is a sentiment of nature, which anticipates the inspired command, "Obey them that have the rule over you, and submit yourselves, for they watch for your souls."

As regards the Roman Emperors, immediately on their becoming Christians, their exaltation of the hierarchy was in proportion to its abject condition in the heathen period.

Grateful converts felt that they could not do too much in its honour and service. Emperors bowed the head before the Bishops, kissed their hands and asked their blessing. When Constantine entered into the presence of the assembled Prelates at Nicæa, his eyes fell, the colour mounted up into his cheek, and his mien was that of a suppliant; he would not sit, till the Bishops bade him, and he kissed the wounds of the Confessors. He set the example for the successors of his power, nor did the Bishops decline such honours. Emperors' wives served them at table; when they did wrong, they did penance and asked forgiveness. When they quarrelled with them, and would banish them, their hand trembled when they came to sign the order, and refused to do its office, and after various attempts they gave up their purpose. Soldiers raised to sovereignty asked their recognition and were refused it. Cities under imperial displeasure sought their intervention, and the master of thirty legions found himself powerless to withstand the feeble voice of some aged travel-stained stranger.

Laws were passed in favour of the Church; Bishops could only be judged by Bishops, and the causes of their clergy were withdrawn from the secular courts. Their sentence was final, as if it were the Emperor's own, and the governors of provinces were bound to put it in execution. Litigants everywhere were allowed the liberty of referring their cause to the tribunal of the Bishops, who, besides, became arbitrators on a large scale in private quarrels; and the public, even heathens, wished it so. St. Ambrose was sometimes so taken up with business of this sort, that he had time for nothing else. St. Austin and Theodoret both complain of the weight of such secular engagements, as forced upon them by the importunity of the people. Nor was this all; the Emperors showed their belief in the divinity of the Church and of its creed by acts of what we should now call persecution. Jews were forbidden to proselytize a Christian; Christians were forbidden to become pagans; pagan rites were abolished, the books of heretics and infidels were burned wholesale; their chapels were razed to the ground, and even their private meetings were made illegal.

These characteristics of the convert Empire were the immediate, some of them the logical, consequences, of its new faith. Had not the Emperors honoured Christianity in its ministers and in its precepts, they would not properly have deserved the name of converts. Nor was it unreasonable in litigants voluntarily to frequent the episcopal tribunals, if they got justice done to them there better than in the civil courts. As to the prohibition of heretical meetings, I cannot get myself quite to believe that Pagans, Marcionites, and Manichees had much tenderness of conscience in their religious profession, or were wounded seriously by the Imperial rescript to their disadvantage. Many of these sects were of a most immoral character, whether in doctrine or practice ; others were forms of witchcraft ; often they were little better than paganism. The Novatians certainly stand on higher ground ; but on the whole, it would be most unjust to class such wild, impure, inhuman rites with even the most extravagant and grotesque of American sectaries now. They could entertain no bitter feeling that injustice was done them in their repression. They did not make free thought or private judgment their watch words. The populations of the Empire did not rise in revolt when its religion was changed. There were two broad conditions which accompanied the grant of all this ecclesiastical power and privilege, and made the exercise of it possible ; first, that the people consented to it, secondly, that it was enforced by the law of the Empire. High and low opened the door to it. The Church of course would say that such prerogatives were rightfully hers, as being at least congruous grants made to her, on the part of the State, in return for the benefits which she bestowed upon it. It was her right to demand them, and the State's duty to concede them. This seems to have been the basis of the new state of society. And in fact these prerogatives were in force and in exercise all through those troublous centuries which followed the break-up of the Imperial sway : and, though the handling of them at length fell into the hands of one see exclusively (on which I shall remark presently), the see of Peter, yet the substance and character of these prerogatives, and the Church's claim to possess them, remained untouched. The change in the internal allocation of power did not affect the existence and the use of the power itself.

Ranke, speaking of this development of ecclesiastical supremacy upon the conversion of the Empire, remarks as follows :

" It appears to me that this was the result of an internal necessity. The rise of Christianity involved the liberation of religion from all political elements. From this followed the growth of a distinct ecclesiastical class with a peculiar constitution. In this separation of the Church from the State consists, perhaps, the greatest, the most pervading and influential peculiarity of all Christian times. The spiritual and secular powers may come into near contact, may even stand in the closest community ; but they can be thoroughly incorporated only at rare conjunctures and for a short period. Their mutual relations, their position with regard to each other, form, from this time forward, one of the most important considerations in all history."—*The Popes*, vol. i., p. 10, *transl.*

§ 3. The Papal Church.

Now we come to the distinctive doctrine of the Catholic Religion, the doctrine which separates us from all other denominations of Christians however near they may approach to us in other respects, the claims of the see of Rome, which have given occasion to Mr. Gladstone's Pamphlet and to the remarks which I am now making upon it. Of those rights, prerogatives, privileges, and duties, which I have been surveying in the ancient Church, the Pope is the heir. I shall dwell now upon this point, as far as it is to my purpose to do so, not treating it theologically (else I must define and prove from Scripture and the Fathers the "Primatus jure divino Romani Pontificis"), but historically, because Mr. Gladstone appeals to history. Instead of treating it theologically I wish to look with (as it were) secular, or even non-Catholic eyes at the powers claimed during the last thousand years by the Pope—that is, only as they lie in the nature of the case, and in the surface of the facts which come before us in history.

1. I say then the Pope is the heir of the Ecumenical Hierarchy of the fourth century, as being, what I may call, heir by default. No one else claims or exercises its rights or its duties. Is it possible to consider the Patriarch of Moscow or of Constantinople, heir to the historical pretensions of St. Ambrose or St. Martin? Does any Anglican Bishop for the last 300 years recall to our minds the image of St. Basil? Well, then, has all that ecclesiastical power, which makes such a show in the Christian Empire, simply vanished, or, if not, where is it to be found? I wish Protestants would throw themselves into our minds upon this point; I am not holding an argument with them; I am only wishing them to understand where we stand and how we look at things. There is this great difference of belief between us and them: they do not believe that Christ set up a visible society, or rather

kingdom, for the propagation and maintenance of His religion, for a necessary home and refuge of His people ; but we do. We know the kingdom is still on earth : where is it ? If all that can be found of it is what can be discerned at Constantinople or Canterbury, I say, it has disappeared ; and either there was a radical corruption of Christianity from the first, or Christianity came to an end, in proportion as the type of the Nicene Church faded out of the world : for all that we know of Christianity, in ancient history, as a concrete fact, is the Church of Athanasius and his fellows : it is nothing else historically but that bundle of phenomena, that combination of claims, prerogatives, and corresponding acts, some of which I have recounted above. There is no help for it ; we cannot take as much as we please, and no more, of an institution which has a monadic existence. We must either give up the belief in the Church as a divine institution altogether, or we must recognize it in that communion of which the Pope is the head. With him alone and round about him are found the claims, the prerogatives, and duties which we identify with the kingdom set up by Christ. We must take things as they are ; to believe in a Church, is to believe in the Pope. And thus this belief in the Pope and his attributes, which seems so monstrous to Protestants, is bound up with our being Catholics at all ; as our Catholicism is with our Christianity. There is nothing then of wanton opposition to the powers that be, no dinning of novelties in their startled ears in what is often unjustly called Ultramontane doctrine ; there is no pernicious servility to the Pope in our admission of his pretensions. I say, we cannot help ourselves—Parliament may deal as harshly with us as it will ; we should not believe in the Church at all, unless we believed in its visible head.

So it is ; the course of ages has fulfilled the prophecy and promise, " Thou art Peter, and upon this rock I will build My Church ; and whatsoever thou shalt bind on earth, shall be bound in heaven, and whatsoever thou shalt loose on earth shall be loosed in heaven." That which in substance was possessed by the Nicene Hierarchy, that the Pope claims now. I do not wish to put difficulties in my way ;

but I cannot conceal or smooth over what I believe to be a simple truth, though the avowal of it will be very unwelcome to Protestants, and, as I fear, to some Catholics. However, I do not call upon another to believe all that I believe on the subject myself. I declare it, as my own judgment, that the prerogatives, such as, and, in the way in which, I have described them in substance, which the Church had under the Roman Power, those she claims now, and never, never will relinquish; claims them, not as having received them from a dead Empire, but partly by the direct endowment of her Divine Master, and partly as being a legitimate outcome of that endowment; claims them, but not except from Catholic populations, not as if accounting the more sublime of them to be of every-day use, but holding them as a protection or remedy in great emergencies or on supreme occasions, when nothing else will serve, as extraordinary and solemn acts of her religious sovereignty. And our Lord, seeing what would be brought about by human means, even had He not willed it, and recognizing, from the laws which He Himself had imposed upon human society, that no large community could be strong which had no head, spoke the word in the beginning, as He did to Judah, "Thou art he whom thy brethren shall praise," and then left it to the course of events to fulfil it.

2. Mr. Gladstone ought to have chosen another issue for attack upon us, than the Pope's power. His real difficulty lies deeper; as little permission as he allows to the Pope, would he allow to any ecclesiastic who would wield the weapons of St. Ambrose and St. Augustine. That concentration of the Church's powers which history brings before us should not be the object of his special indignation. It is not the existence of a Pope, but of a Church, which is his aversion. It is the powers, and not their distribution and allocation in the ecclesiastical body which he writes against. A triangle or parallelogram is the same in its substance and nature, whichever side is made its base. "The Pontiffs," says Mr. Bowden, who writes as an Anglican, "exalted to the kingly throne of St. Peter, did not so much claim new privileges for themselves, as deprive their episcopal brethren of privi-

leges originally common to the hierarchy. Even the title
by which those autocratical prelates, in the plenitude o
their power, delighted to style themselves, 'Summus Sacer
dos,' 'Pontifex Maximus,' 'Vicarius Christi,' 'Papa' itself
had, nearer to the primitive times, been the honourable
appellations of every bishop ; as "Sedes Apostolica" had
been the description of every Bishop's throne. The ascription of these titles, therefore, to the Pope only gave to the
terms new force, because that ascription became exclusive ;
because, that is, the bishops in general were stripped of
honours, to which their claims were as well founded as those
of their Roman brother, who became, by the change, not so
strictly universal as sole Bishop." (*Greg.* vii. vol. i. p. 64.)

Say that the Christian polity remained, as history repre-
sents it to us in the fourth century, or that now it was, if
that was possible, to revert to such a state, would politicians
have less trouble with 1800 centres of power than they
have with one ? Instead of one, with traditionary rules, the
trammels of treaties and engagements, public opinion to
consult and manage, the responsibility of great interests,
and the guarantee for his behaviour in his temporal possessions, there would be a legion of ecclesiastics, each bishop
with his following, each independent of the others,
each with his own views, each with extraordinary powers,
each with the risk of misusing them, all over Christendom.
It would be the Anglican theory, made real. It would be
an ecclesiastical communism ; and, if it did not benefit religion, at least it would not benefit the civil power. Take a
small illustration :—what interruption at this time to Parliamentary proceedings, does a small zealous party occasion,
which its enemies call a "mere handful of clergy ;" and
why ? Because its members are responsible for what they
do to God alone and to their conscience as His voice. Even
suppose it was only here or there that episcopal autonomy
was vigorous ; yet consider what zeal is kindled by local interests and national spirit. One John of Tuam, with a Pope's
full apostolic powers, would be a greater trial to successive
ministries than an Ecumenical Bishop at Rome. Parliament
understands this well, for it exclaims against the Sacerdotal

principle. Here, for a second reason, if our Divine Master has given those great powers to the Church, which ancient Christianity testifies, we see why His Providence has also provided that the exercise of them should be concentrated in one see.

But, anyhow, the progress of concentration was not the work of the Pope ; it was brought about by the changes of times and the vicissitudes of nations. It was not his fault that the Vandals swept away the African sees, and the Saracens those of Syria and Asia Minor, or that Constantinople and its dependencies became the creatures of Imperialism, or that France, England, and Germany would obey none but the author of their own Christianity, or that clergy and people at a distance were obstinate in sheltering themselves under the majesty of Rome against their own fierce kings and nobles or imperious bishops, even to the imposing forgeries on the world and on the Pope in justification of their proceedings. All this will be fact, whether the Popes were ambitious or not ; and still it will be fact that the issue of that great change was a great benefit to the whole of Europe. No one but a Master, who was a thousand bishops in himself at once, could have tamed and controlled, as the Pope did, the great and little tyrants of the middle age.

3. This is generally confessed now, even by Protestant historians, viz., that the concentration of ecclesiastical power in those centuries was simply necessary for the civilization of Europe. Of course it does not follow that the benefits rendered then to the European commonwealth by the political supremacy of the Pope, would, if he was still supreme, be rendered in time to come. I have no wish to make assumptions ; yet conclusions short of this will be unfavourable to Mr. Gladstone's denunciation of him. We reap the fruit at this day of his services in the past. With the purpose of showing this I make a rather long extract from Dean Milman's " Latin Christianity ;" he is speaking of the era of Gregory I, and he says, the Papacy. " was the only power which lay not entirely and absolutely prostrate before the disasters of the times—a power which had an inherent

strength, and might resume its majesty. It was this power which was most imperatively required to preserve all which was to survive out of the crumbling wreck of Roman civilization. To Western Christianity was absolutely necessary a centre, standing alone, strong in traditionary reverence, and in acknowledged claims to supremacy. Even the perfect organization of the Christian hierarchy might in all human probability have fallen to pieces in perpetual conflict : it might have degenerated into a half secular feudal caste, with hereditary benefices more and more entirely subservient to the civil authority, a priesthood of each nation or each tribe, gradually sinking to the intellectual or religious level of the nation or tribe. On the rise of a power both controlling and conservative hung, humanly speaking, the life and death of Christianity—of Christianity as a permanent, aggressive, expansive, and, to a certain extent, uniform system. There must be a counterbalance to barbaric force, to the unavoidable anarchy of Teutonism, with its tribal, or at the utmost national independence, forming a host of small, conflicting, antagonistic kingdoms. All Europe would have been what England was under the Octarchy, what Germany was when her emperors were weak ; and even her emperors she owed to Rome, to the Church, to Christianity. Providence might have otherwise ordained ; but it is impossible for man to imagine by what other organising or consolidating force the commonwealth of the Western nations could have grown up to a discordant, indeed, and conflicting league, but still a league, with that unity and conformity of manners, usages, laws, religion, which have made their rivalries, oppugnancies, and even their long ceaseless wars, on the whole to issue in the noblest, highest, most intellectual form of civilization known to man...It is impossible to conceive what had been the confusion, the lawlessness, the chaotic state of the middle ages, without the medieval Papacy ; and of the medieval Papacy the real father is Gregory the Great. In all his predecessors there was much of the uncertainty and indefiniteness of a new dominion. ...Gregory is the Roman altogether merged in the Christian Bishop. It is a Christian dominion, of which he lays the foundations in the Eternal City, not the old Rome, associating Christian influence to her ancient title of sovereignty." (Vol. i., p. 401, 2.)

4. From Gregory I. to Innocent III. is six hundred years ; —a very fair portion of the world's history, to have passed in doing good of primary importance to a whole continent, and that the continent of Europe ; good, by which all nations and their governors, all statesmen and legislatures, are the gainers. And, again, should it not occur to Mr. Gladstone that these services were rendered to mankind by means of those very instruments of power on which he thinks it proper to pour contempt as " rusty tools ?" The right to warn and punish powerful men, to excommunicate kings, to preach aloud truth and justice to the inhabitants of the earth, to denounce immoral doctrines, to strike at rebellion in the garb of heresy, were the very weapons ,by which Europe was brought into a civilized condition ; yet he calls them " rusty tools" which need " refurbishing." Does he wish then that such high expressions of ecclesiastical displeasure, such sharp penalties, should be of daily use ? If they are rusty, because they have been long without using, then have they ever been rusty. Is a Council a rusty tool, because none had been held, till 1870, since the sixteenth century ? or because there had been but nineteen in 1900 years ? How many times is it in the history of Christianity that the Pope has solemnly drawn and exercised his sword upon a king or an emperor ? If an extraordinary weapon must be a rusty tool, I suppose Gregory VII.'s sword was not keen enough for the German Henry ; and the seventh Pius too used a rusty tool in his excommunication of Napoleon. How could Mr. Gladstone ever " fondly think that Rome had disused" her weapons, and that they had hung up as antiquities and curiosities in her celestial armoury,—or, in his own words, as " hideous mummies," p. 46,—when the passage of arms between the great Conqueror and the aged Pope was so close upon his memory ! Would he like to see a mummy come to life again ? That unexpected miracle actually took place in the first years of this century. Gregory was considered to have done an astounding deed in

the middle ages, when he brought Henry, the German Emperor, to do penance and shiver in the snow at Canossa; but Napoleon had his snow-penance too, and that with an actual interposition of Providence in the infliction of it. I describe it in the words of Alison :—

"'What does the Pope mean,' said Napoleon to Eugene, in July, 1807, 'by the threat of excommunicating me? does he think the world has gone back a thousand years? Does he suppose the arms will fall from the hands of my soldiers?' Within two years after these remarkable words were written, the Pope did excommunicate him, in return for the confiscation of his whole dominions, and in less than four years more, the arms did fall from the hands of his soldiers; and the hosts, apparently invincible, which he had collected were dispersed and ruined by the blasts of winter. 'The weapons of the soldiers,' says Segur, in describing the Russian retreat, 'appeared of an insupportable weight to their stiffened arms. During their frequent falls they fell from their hands, and destitute of the power of raising them from the ground, they were left in the snow. They did not throw them away : famine and cold tore them from their grasp.' 'The soldiers could no longer hold their weapons,' says Salgues, 'they fell from the hands even of the bravest and most robust. The muskets dropped from the frozen arms of those who bore them.'" (*Hist.* ch. lx., 9th ed.)

Alison adds—" There is something in these marvellous coincidences beyond the operations of chance, and which even a Protestant historian feels himself bound to mark for the observation of future ages. The world has not gone back a thousand years, but that Being existed with whom a thousand years are as one day, and one day as a thousand years." As He was with Gregory in 1077, so He was with Pius in 1812, and He will be with some future Pope again, when the necessity shall come.

5. In saying this, I am far from saying that Popes are never in the wrong, and are never to be resisted; or that their excommunications always avail. I am not bound to defend the policy or the acts of particular Popes, whether before or after the

great revolt from their authority in the 16th century. There
is no reason that I should contend, and I do not contend, for
instance, that they at all times have understood our own
people, our national character and resources, and our position in Europe ; or that they have never suffered from bad
counsellors or misinformation.   I say this the more freely,
because Urban VIII., about the year 1641 or 1642,
blamed the policy of some Popes of the preceding century
in their dealings with our country.*

But, whatever we are bound to allow to Mr. Gladstone
on this head, that does not warrant the passionate invective
against the Holy See and us individually, which he has carried on through sixty-four pages. What we have a manifest
right to expect from him is lawyer-like exactness and logical consecutiveness in his impeachment of us.   The heavier
that is, the less does it need the exaggerations of a great
orator.   If the Pope's conduct towards us three centuries
ago has righteously wiped out the memory of his earlier
benefits, yet he should have a fair trial.   The more intoxi-
cating was his solitary greatness, when it was in the zenith,
the greater consideration should be shown towards him in his
present temporal humiliation, when concentration of ecclesiastical functions in one man, does but make him, in the presence
of the haters of Catholicism, what a Roman Emperor con-
templated, when he wished all his subjects had but one neck
that he might destroy them by one blow.   Surely, in the
trial of so august a criminal, one might have hoped, at least,
to have found gravity and measure in language, and calm-
ness in tone—not a pamphlet written as if on impulse, in defence of an incidental parenthesis in a previous publication,

---

* "When he was urged to excommunicate the Kings of France and
Sweden, he made answer, 'We may declare them excommunicate, as Pius V. declared Queen Elizabeth of England, and before him
Clement VII. the King of England, Henry VIII. . . but with what
success? The whole world can tell. We yet bewail it with tears of
blood. Wisdom does not teach us to imitate Pius V. or Clement VII.,
but Paul V. who, in the beginning, being many times urged by the Spa-
niards to excommunicate James King of England, never would consent
to it'" (State Paper Office, *Italy*, 1641—1662). *Vide* Mr. Simpson's very
able and careful life of Campion, 1867, p. 371.

and then, after having been multiplied in 22,000 copies, appealing to the lower classes in the shape of a sixpenny tract, the lowness of the price indicating the width of the circulation. Surely Nana Sahib will have more justice done to him by the English people, than has been shown to the Father of European civilization.

6. I have been referring to the desolate state in which the Holy See has been cast during the last years, such that the Pope, humanly speaking, is at the mercy of his enemies, and morally a prisoner in his palace. A state of such secular feebleness cannot last for ever; sooner or later there will be, in the divine mercy, a change for the better, and the Vicar of Christ will no longer be a mark for insult and indignity. But one thing, except by an almost miraculous interposition, cannot be; and that is, a return to the universal religious sentiment, the public opinion, of the medieval time. The Pope himself calls those centuries "the ages of faith." Such endemic faith may certainly be decreed for some future time; but, as far as we have the means of judging at present, centuries must run out first. Even in the fourth century the ecclesiastical privileges, claimed on the one hand, granted on the other, came into effect more or less under two conditions, that they were recognized by public law, and that they had the consent of the Christian populations. Is there any chance whatever, except by miracles which were not granted then, that the public law and the inhabitants of Europe will allow the Pope that exercise of his rights, which they allowed him as a matter of course in the 11th and 12th centuries? If the whole world will at once answer No, it is surely inopportune to taunt us with the acts of medieval Popes in the case of certain princes and nobles, when the sentiment of Europe was radically Papal. How does the past bear upon the present in this matter? Yet Mr. Gladstone is in earnest alarm, earnest with the earnestness which distinguishes him as a statesman, at the harm which society may receive from the Pope, at a time when the Pope can do nothing. He grants (p. 46) that "the fears are visionary . . that either foreign foe or domestic treason can, at the bidding of the Court of Rome,

disturb these peaceful shores; " he allows that "in the middle ages the Popes contended, not by direct action of fleets and armies," but mainly " by interdicts," p. 35. Yet, because men then believed in interdicts, though now they don't, therefore the civil Power is to be roused against the Pope. But his *animus* is bad ; his *animus!* what can *animus* do without matter to work upon ?   Mere *animus*, like big words, breaks no bones.

As if to answer Mr. Gladstone by anticipation, and to allay his fears, the Pope made a declaration three years ago on the subject, which, strange to say, Mr. Gladstone quotes without perceiving that it tells against the very argument, which he brings it to corroborate ;—that is, except as the Pope's *animus* goes.   Doubtless he would wish to have the place in the political world which his predecessors had, because it was given to him by Providence, and is conducive to the highest interests of mankind ; but he distinctly tells us that he has not got it, and cannot have it, till a time comes, of the prospect of which we are as good judges as he can be, and which we say cannot come, at least for centuries. He speaks of what is his highest political power, that of interposing in the quarrel between a prince and his subjects, and of declaring upon appeal made to him from them, that the Prince had or had not forfeited their allegiance. This power, most rarely exercised, and on very extraordinary occasions, and without any aid of infallibility in the exercise of it, any more than the civil power possesses that aid, it is not necessary for any Catholic to believe ; and I suppose, comparatively speaking, few Catholics do believe it ; to be honest, I must say, I do ; that is, under the conditions which the Pope himself lays down in the declaration to which I have referred, his answer to the address of the Academia. He speaks of his right " to depose sovereigns, and release the people from the obligation of loyalty, a right which had undoubtedly sometimes been exercised in crucial circumstances," and he says, " This right (*diritto*) in those ages of faith,—(which discerned in the Pope, what he is, that is to say, the Supreme Judge of Christianity, and recognized the advantages of his tribunal in the great contests of peoples and sovereigns)—was freely extended,—(aided indeed as a matter of duty by the public law (*diritto*) and by the common consent of peoples)—to the most important (*i piu gravi*) interests of states and their rulers." (Guardian, *Nov.* 11, 1874).

Now let us observe how the Pope restrains the exercise of this right. He calls it his right—that is, in the sense in which right in one party is correlative with duty in the other, so that, when the duty is not observed, the right cannot be brought into exercise ; and this is precisely what he goes on to intimate ; for he lays down the conditions of of that exercise. First it can only be exercised in rare and critical circumstances (*supreme circonstanze, i più gravi interessi*). Next he refers to his being the supreme judge of Christianity, and to his decision as coming from a tribunal ; his prerogative then is not a mere arbitrary power, but must be exercised by a process of law and a formal examination of the case, and in the presence and the hearing of the two parties interested in it. Also in this limitation is implied that the Pope's definitive sentence involves an appeal to the supreme standard of right and wrong, the moral law, as its basis and rule, and must contain the definite reasons on which it decides in favour of the one party or the other. Thirdly, the exercise of this right is limited to the ages of faith ; ages which, on the one hand, inscribed it among the provisions of the *jus publicum*, and on the other so fully recognized the benefits it conferred, as to be able to enforce it by the common consent of the peoples. These last words should be dwelt on : it is no consent which is merely local, as of one country, of Ireland or of Belgium, if that were probable ; but a united consent of various nations, of Europe, for instance, as a commonwealth, of which the Pope was the head. Thirty years ago we heard much of the Pope being made the head of an Italian confederation : no word came from England against such an arrangement. It was possible, because the members of it were all of one religion ; and in like manner a European commonwealth would be reasonable, if Europe were of one religion. Lastly, the Pope declares with indignation that a Pope is not infallible in the exercise of this right ; such a notion is an invention of the enemy ; he calls it " malicious."

§ 4. DIVIDED ALLEGIANCE.

But one attribute the Church has, and the Pope as head of the Church, whether he be in high estate, as this world goes, or not, whether he has temporal possessions or not, whether he is in honour or dishonour, whether he is at home or driven about, whether those special claims of which I have spoken are allowed or not,—and that is Sovereignty. As God has sovereignty, though He may be disobeyed or disowned, so has His Vicar upon earth ; and further than this, since Catholic populations are found everywhere, he ever will be in fact lord of a vast empire ; as large in numbers, as far spreading as the British ; and all. his acts are sure to be such as are in keeping with the position of one who is thus supremely exalted.

I beg not to be interrupted here, as many a reader will interrupt me in his thoughts, for I am using these words, not at random, but as the commencement of a long explanation, and, in a certain sense, limitation, of what I have hitherto been saying concerning the Church's and the Pope's power. To this task the remaining pages, which I have to address to your Grace, will be directed; and I trust that it will turn out, when I come to the end of them, that, by first stating fully what the Pope's claims are, I shall be able most clearly to show what he does not claim.

Now the key-note of Mr. Gladstone's Pamphlet is this :—that, since the Pope claims infallibility in faith and morals, and since there are no " departments and functions of human life which do not and cannot fall within the domain of morals," p. 36, and since he claims also " the domain of all that concerns the government and discipline of the Church," and moreover, " claims the power of determining the limits of those domains," and " does not sever them, by any acknowledged or intelligible line from the

domains of civil duty and allegiance," p. 45, therefore
Catholics are moral and mental slaves, and "every convert and member of the Pope's Church places his loyalty
and civil duty at the mercy of another," p. 45.

I admit Mr. Gladstone's premisses, but I reject his
conclusion; and now I am going to show why I reject it.

In doing this, I shall, with him, put aside for the
present the Pope's prerogative of infallibility in general
enunciations, whether of faith or morals, and confine myself to the consideration of his authority (in respect to
which he is not infallible) in matters of daily conduct, and of
our duty of obedience to him. "There is something wider
still, "he says, (than the claim of infallibility,) "and that is
the claim to an ¹Absolute and entire Obedience," p. 37.
"Little does it matter to me, whether my Superior claims
infallibility, so long as he is entitled to demand and exact
conformity," p. 39. He speaks of a third province being
opened, "not indeed to the abstract assertion of Infallibility, but to the far more practical and decisive demand of
Absolute Obedience," p. 41, "the Absolute Obedience, at
the peril of salvation, of every member of his communion,"
p. 42.

Now, I proceed to examine this large, direct, religious
sovereignty of the Pope, both in its relation to his subjects, and to the Civil Power; but first, I beg to be
allowed to say just one word on the principle of obedience
itself, that is, by way of inquiry, whether it is or is not
now a religious duty.

Is there then such a duty at all as obedience to ecclesiastical authority now? or is it one of those obsolete
ideas, which are swept away, as unsightly cobwebs, by the
New Civilization? Scripture says, "Remember them
which have the *rule* over you, who have spoken unto you
the word of God, whose faith follow." And, "*Obey* them
that have the *rule* over you, and *submit yourselves*; for
they watch *for your souls*, as they that must give account,
that they may do it with joy and not with grief; for that
is unprofitable for you." The margin in the Protestant

Version reads, "those who are your *guides;*" and the word may also be translated "leaders." Well, as rulers, or guides and leaders, whichever word be right, they are to be *obeyed.* Now Mr. Gladstone dislikes our way of fulfilling this precept, whether as regards our choice of ruler and leader, or our "Absolute Obedience" to him ; but he does not give us his own. Is there any liberalistic reading of the Scripture passage ? Or are the words only for the benefit of the poor and ignorant, not for the *Schola* (as it may be called) of political and periodical writers, not for individual members of Parliament, not for statesmen and Cabinet ministers, and people of Progress ? Which party then is the more "Scriptural," those who recognize and carry out in their conduct texts like these, or those who don't ? May not we Catholics claim some mercy from Mr. Gladstone, though we be faulty in the object and the manner of our obedience, since in a lawless day an object and a manner of obedience we have ? Can we be blamed, if, arguing from those texts which say that ecclesiastical authority comes from above, we obey it in that one form in which alone we find it on earth, in that only person who claims it of us, among all the notabilities of this nineteenth century into which we have been born ? The Pope has no rival in his claim upon us ; nor is it our doing that his claim has been made and allowed for centuries upon centuries, and that it was he who made the Vatican decrees, and not they him. If we give him up, to whom shall we go ? Can we dress up any civil functionary in the vestments of divine authority ? Can I, for instance, follow the faith, can I put my soul into the hands, of our gracious Sovereign ? or of the Archbishop of Canterbury ? or of the Bishop of Lincoln, albeit he is not broad and low, but high ? Catholics have "done what they could,"—all that any one could : and it should be Mr. Gladstone's business, before telling us that we are slaves, because we obey the Pope, first of all to tear away those texts from the Bible.

With this preliminary remark, I proceed to consider whether the Pope's authority is either a slavery to his subjects, or a menace to the Civil Power ; and first, as to his power over his flock.

1. Mr. Gladstone says that "the Pontiff declares to belong to him the *supreme direction* of Catholics in respect to all duty," p. 37. Supreme direction; true, but " supreme " is not " minute," nor does " direction " mean supervision or " management." Take the parallel of human law ; the Law is *supreme*, and the Law *directs* our conduct under the manifold circumstances in which we have to act, and must be absolutely obeyed ; but who therefore says that the Law has the " supreme direction" of us ? The State, as well as the Church, has the power at its will of imposing laws upon us, laws bearing on our moral duties, our daily conduct, affecting our actions in various ways, and circumscribing our liberties ; yet no one would say that the Law, after all, with all its power in the abstract and its executive vigour in fact, interferes either with our comfort or our conscience. There are numberless laws about property, landed and personal, titles, tenures, trusts, wills, covenants, contracts, partnerships, money transactions, life-insurances, taxes, trade, navigation, education, sanitary measures, trespasses, nuisances, all in addition to the criminal law. Law, to apply Mr. Gladstone's words, " is the shadow that cleaves to us, go where we will." Moreover, it varies year after year, and refuses to give any pledge of fixedness or finality. Nor can any one tell what restraint is to come next, perhaps painful personally to himself. Nor are its enactments easy of interpretation ; for actual cases, with the speeches and opinions of counsel, and the decisions of judges, must prepare the raw material, as it proceeds from the legislature, before it can be rightly understood ; so that " the glorious uncertainty of the Law " has become a proverb. And, after all, no one is sure of escaping its penalties without the assistance of lawyers, and that in such private and personal matters that the lawyers are, as by an imperative duty, bound to a secrecy which even courts of justice respect. And then, besides the Statute Law, there is the common and traditional ; and, below this, usage. Is not all this enough to try the temper of a free-born Englishman, and to make him cry out with Mr. Gladstone, " Three-fourths of my life are handed

over to the Law; I care not to ask if there be dregs or
tatters of human life, such as can escape from the description and boundary of Parliamentary tyranny?" Yet,
though we may dislike it, though we may at times suffer
from it ever so much, who does not see that the thraldom
and irksomeness is nothing compared with the great blessings which the Constitution and Legislature secure to us?

Such is the jurisdiction which the Law exercises over us.
What rule does the Pope claim which can be compared to
its strong and its long arm? What interference with our
liberty of judging and acting in our daily work, in our
course of life, comes to us from him? Really, at first sight,
I have not known where to look for instances of his actual
interposition in our private affairs, for it is our routine of
personal duties about which I am now speaking. Let us
see how we stand in this matter.

We are guided in our ordinary duties by the books of
moral theology, which are drawn up by theologians of
authority and experience, as an instruction for our Confessors.
These books are based on the three Christian foundations
of Faith, Hope, and Charity, on the Ten Commandments,
and on the six Precepts of the Church, which relate to
the observance of Sunday, of fast days, of confession and
communion, and, in one shape or other, to paying tithes.
A great number of possible cases are noted under these
heads, and in difficult questions a variety of opinions are
given, with plain directions, when it is that private Catholics are at liberty to choose for themselves whatever answer
they like best, and when they are bound to follow some
one of them in particular. Reducible as these directions
in detail are to the few and simple heads which I have
mentioned, they are little more than reflexions and memo-
randa of our moral sense, unlike the positive enactments of
the Legislature ; and, on the whole, present to us no difficulty—though now and then some critical question may
arise, and some answer may be given (just as by the private
conscience) which it is difficult to us or painful to accept.
And again, cases may occur now and then, when our private
judgment differs from what is set down in theological

works, but even then it does not follow at once that our private judgment must give way, for those books are no utterance of Papal authority.

And this is the point to which I am coming. So little does the Pope come into this whole system of moral theology by which (as by our conscience) our lives are regulated, that the weight of his hand upon us, as private men, is absolutely unappreciable. I have had a difficulty where to find a measure or guage of his interposition. At length I have looked through Busenbaum's "Medulla," to ascertain what light such a book would throw upon the question. It is a book of casuistry for the use of Confessors, running to 700 pages, and is a large repository of answers made by various theologians on points of conscience, and generally of duty. It was first published in 1645—my own edition is of 1844—and in the latter are marked those propositions, bearing on subjects treated in it, which have been condemned by Popes in the intermediate 200 years. On turning over the pages I find they are in all between 50 and 60. This list includes matters sacramental, ritual, ecclesiastical, monastic, and disciplinarian, as well as moral, —relating to the duties of ecclesiastics and regulars, of parish priests, and of professional men, as well as of private Catholics. And the condemnations relate for the most part to mere occasional details of duty, and are in reprobation of the lax or wild notions of speculative casuists, so that they are rather restraints upon theologians than upon laymen. For instance, the following are some of the propositions condemned :—" The ecclesiastic, who on a certain day is hindered from saying Matins and Lauds, is not bound to say, if he can, the remaining hours ;" " Where there is good cause, it is lawful to swear without the purpose of swearing, whether the matter is of light or grave moment;" " Domestics may steal from their masters, in compensation for their service, which they think greater than their wages ;" " It is lawful for a public man to kill an opponent, who tries to fasten a calumny upon him, if he cannot otherwise escape the ignominy." I have taken these instances at random. It must be granted, I think, that in the long

course of 200 years the amount of the Pope's authoritative
enunciations has not been such as to press heavily on the
back of the private Catholic.   He leaves us surely far
more than that "one fourth of the department of conduct," which Mr. Gladstone allows us.   Indeed, if my
account and specimens of his sway over us in morals be
correct, I do not see what he takes away at all from our
private consciences.

Mr. Gladstone says that the Pope virtually claims
to himself the wide domain of conduct, and *therefore* that we are his slaves :— let us see if another
illustration or parallel will not show this to be a
non-sequitur. Suppose a man, who is in the midst
of various and important lines of business, has a medical adviser, in whom he has full confidence, as knowing
well his constitution.   This adviser keeps a careful and
anxious eye upon him ; and, as an honest man, says to
him, "You must not go off on a journey to-day," or "you
must take some days' rest," or "you must attend to your
diet." Now, this is not a fair parallel to the Pope's hold upon
us ; for he does not speak to us personally but to all, and in
speaking definitively on ethical subjects, what he propounds
must relate to things good and bad in themselves, not to
things accidental, changeable, and of mere expedience ; so
that the argument which I am drawing from the case of a
medical adviser is *à fortiori* in its character.   However, I say
that, though a medical man exercises a "supreme direction"
of those who put themselves under him, yet we do not therefore say, even of him, that he interferes with our daily conduct, and that we are his slaves.   He certainly does thwart
many of our wishes and purposes ; in a true sense we are
at his mercy : he may interfere any day, suddenly ; he
will not, he cannot, draw any line between his action and
our action.   The same journey, the same press of business,
the same indulgence at table, which he passes over one
year, he sternly forbids the next.   If Mr. Gladstone's
argument is good, he has a finger in all the commercial
transactions of the great merchant or financier who has
chosen him.   But surely there is a simple fallacy here.

Mr. Gladstone asks us whether our political and civil life is not at the Pope's mercy; every act, he says, of at least three-quarters of the day, is under his control. No, not *every*, but *any*, and this is all the difference—that is, we have no guarantee given us that there will never be a case, when the Pope's general utterances may come to have a bearing upon some personal act of ours. In the same way we are all of us in this age under the control of public opinion and the public prints; nay, much more intimately so. Journalism can be and is very personal; and, when it is in the right, more powerful just now than any Pope; yet we do not go into fits, as if we were slaves, because we are under a *surveillance* much more like tyranny than any sway, so indirect, so practically limited, so gentle, as his is.

But it seems the cardinal point of our slavery lies, not simply in the domain of morals, but in the Pope's general authority over us in all things whatsoever. This count in his indictment Mr. Gladstone founds on a passage in the third chapter of the *Pastor æternus*, in which the Pope, speaking of the Pontifical jurisdiction, says:—" Towards it (erga quam) pastors and people of whatsoever rite or dignity, each and all, are bound by the duty of hierarchical subordination and true obedience, not only in matters which pertain to faith and morals, but also in those which pertain to the *discipline* and the *regimen* of the Church spread throughout the world; so that, unity with the Roman Pontiff (both of communion and of profession of the same faith) being preserved, the Church of Christ may be one flock under one supreme Shepherd. This is the doctrine of Catholic truth, from which no one can deviate without loss of faith and salvation."

On Mr. Gladstone's use of this passage I observe first, that he leaves out a portion of it which has much to do with the due understanding of it (ita ut custoditâ, &c.) Next, he speaks of " *absolute* obedience" so often, that any reader, who had not the passage before him, would think that the word " absolute " was the Pope's word, not his. Thirdly, three times (at pp. 38, 41, and 42) does he make the Pope say that no one can *disobey* him without risking his salva-

tion, whereas what the Pope does say is, that no one can
disbelieve the *duty* of obedience and unity without such
risk.   And fourthly, in order to carry out this false sense, or
rather to hinder its being evidently impossible, he mis-
translates, p. 38, "doctrina" (Hæc est doctrina) by the
word "rule."

But his chief attack is directed to the words "dis-
ciplina" and "regimen."   "Thus," he says, "are swept
into the Papal net whole multitudes of facts, whole systems of government, prevailing, though in different degrees, in every country of the world," p. 41.   That is, *disci-
plina* and *regimen* are words of such lax, vague, indetermi-
nate meaning, that under them any matters can be slipped
in which may be required for the Pope's purpose in this or
that country, such as, to take Mr. Gladstone's instances,
blasphemy, poor-relief, incorporation and mortmain ; as if
no definitions were contained in our theological and ecclesiastical works of words in such common use, and as if in
consequence the Pope was at liberty to give them any sense
of his own.   As to discipline, Fr. Perrone says "Discipline
comprises the exterior worship of God, the liturgy, sacred
rites, psalmody, the administration of the sacraments, the
canonical form of sacred elections and the institution of
ministers, vows, feast-days, and the like ;" all of them
(observe) matters internal to the Church, and without any
relation to the Civil Power and civil affairs.   Perrone adds,
"Ecclesiastical discipline is a practical and external rule,
prescribed by the Church, in order to retain the faithful in
their *faith*, and the more easily lead them on to *eternal
happiness*," *Prœl. Theol.* t. 2, p. 381, 2nd ed., 1841.   Thus
discipline is in no sense a political instrument, except as
the profession of our faith may accidentally become political.   In the same sense Zallinger :   "The Roman Pontiff
has by divine right the power of passing universal laws per-
taining to the *discipline* of the Church ; for instance, to
divine worship, sacred rites, the ordination and manner of
life of the clergy, the order of the ecclesiastical regimen,
and the right administration of the temporal possessions of
the church."—*Jur. Eccles.*, lib. i., t. 2, § 121.

So too the word "regimen" has a definite meaning, relating to a matter strictly internal to the Church; it means government, or the mode or form of government, or the course of government, and, as, in the intercourse of nation with nation, the nature of a nation's government, whether monarchical or republican, does not come into question, so the constitution of the Church simply belongs to its nature, not to its external action. There are indeed aspects of the Church which involve relations toward secular powers and to nations, as, for instance, its missionary office; but regimen has relation to one of its internal characteristics, viz., its form of government, whether we call it a pure monarchy or with others a monarchy tempered by aristocracy. Thus Tournely says, "Three kinds of regimen or government are set down by philosophers, monarchy, aristocracy, and democracy." *Theol.*, t. 2, p. 100. Bellarmine says the same, *Rom. Pont.* i. 2; and Perrone takes it for granted, *ibid.* pp. 70, 71.

Now, why does the Pope speak at this time of regimen and discipline ?   He tells us, in that portion of the sentence, which, thinking it of no account, Mr. Gladstone has omitted. The Pope tells us that all Catholics should recollect their duty of obedience to him, not only in faith and morals, but in such matters of regimen and discipline as belong to the universal Church, " so that unity with the Roman Pontiff, both of communion and of profession of the same faith being preserved, the Church of Christ may be one flock under one supreme Shepherd." I consider this passage to be especially aimed at Nationalism : " Recollect," the Pope seems to say, " the Church is one, and that, not only in faith and morals, for schismatics may profess as much as this, but one, wherever it is, all over the world; and not only one, but one and the same, bound together by its one regimen and discipline, and by the same regimen and discipline,—the same rites, the same sacraments, the same usages, and the same one Pastor ; and in these bad times it is necessary for all Catholics to recollect, that this doctrine of the Church's individuality and, as it were, personality, is not a mere received opinion or understanding, which

may be entertained or not, as we please, but is a funda-
mental, necessary truth." This being, speaking under correction, the drift of the passage, I observe that the words
" spread throughout the world" or "universal" are so far
from turning "discipline and regimen" into what Mr.
Gladstone calls a " net," that they contract the range of
both of them, not including, as he would have it, "marriage" here, "blasphemy" there, and "poor-relief" in a third
country, but noting and specifying that one and the same
structure of laws, rites, rules of government, independency,
everywhere, of which the Pope himself is the centre and
life. And surely this is what every one of us will say with
the Pope, who is not an Erastian, and who believes that
the Gospel is no mere philosophy thrown upon the world
at large, no mere quality of mind and thought, no mere
beautiful and deep sentiment or subjective opinion, but a
substantive message from above, guarded and preserved in
a visible polity.

2. And now I am naturally led on to speak of the
Pope's supreme authority, such as I have described it, in
its bearing towards the Civil Power all over the world,—
various, as the Church is invariable,—a power which as
truly comes from God, as his own does.

That collisions can take place between the Holy See
and national governments the history of fifteen hundred
years teaches us ; also, that on both sides there may occur
grievous mistakes. But my question all along lies, not with
"quicquid delirant reges," but with what, under the circumstance of such a collision, is the duty of those who are
both children of the Pope and subjects of the Civil Power.
As to the duty of the Civil Power, I have already intimated in my first section, that it should treat the Holy
See as an independent sovereign, and if this rule had been
observed, the difficulty to Catholics in a country not Catholic, would be most materially lightened. Great Britain
recognizes and is recognized by the United States ; the
two powers have ministers at each other's courts ; here is
one standing prevention of serious quarrels. Misunderstandings between the two co-ordinate powers may arise ; but there

follow explanations, removals of the causes of offence, acts of restitution. In actual collisions, there are conferences, compromises, arbitrations. Now the point to observe here is, that in such cases neither party gives up its abstract rights, but neither party practically insists on them. And each party thinks itself in the right in the particular case, protests against any other view, but still concedes. Neither party says, "I will not make it up with you, till you draw an intelligible line between your domain and mine." I suppose in the Geneva arbitration, though we gave way, we still thought that, in our conduct in the American civil war, we had acted within our rights. I say all this in answer to Mr. Gladstone's challenge to us to draw the line between the Pope's domain and the State's domain in civil or political questions. Many a private American, I suppose, lived in London and Liverpool, all through the correspondence between our Foreign Office and the government of the United States, and Mr. Gladstone never addressed any expostulation to them, or told them they had lost their moral freedom because they took part with their own government. The French, when their late war began, did sweep their German sojourners out of France, (the number, as I recollect, was very great,) but they were not considered to have done themselves much credit by such an act. When we went to war with Russia, the English in St. Petersburg made an address, I think to the Emperor, asking for his protection, and he gave it;—I don't suppose they pledged themselves to the Russian view of the war, nor would he have called them slaves instead of patriots, if they had refused to do so. Suppose England were to send her Ironclads to support Italy against the Pope and his allies, English Catholics would be very indignant, they would take part with the Pope before the war began, they would use all constitutional means to hinder it; but who believes that, when they were once in the war, their action would be anything else than prayers and exertions for a termination of it? What reason is there for saying that they would commit themselves to any step of a treasonable nature, any more than loyal Germans, had they been allowed to remain in France? Yet, because those Germans would not relinquish their allegiance to their country, Mr. Gladstone, were he consistent, would at once send them adrift.

Of course it will be said that in these cases, there is no double allegiance, and again that the German government did not call upon them, as the Pope might call upon English Catholics, nay command them, to take a side; but my argument at least shows this, that till there comes to us a special, direct command from the Pope to oppose our country, we need not be said to have "placed our loyalty and civil duty at the mercy of another," p. 45. It is strange that a great statesman, versed in the new and true philosophy of compromise, instead of taking a practical view of the actual situation, should proceed against us, like a Professor in the schools, with the "parade" of his "relentless" (and may I add "rusty"?) "logic," p. 23.

I say, *till* the Pope told us to exert ourselves for his cause in a quarrel with this country, as in the time of the Armada, we need not attend to an abstract and hypothetical difficulty:—then and not till then. I add, as before, that, if the Holy See were frankly recognized by England, as other Sovereign Powers are, direct quarrels between the two powers would in this age of the world be rare indeed; and still rarer, their becoming so energetic and urgent as to descend into the heart of the community, and to disturb the consciences and the family unity of private Catholics.

But now, lastly, let us suppose one of these extraordinary cases of direct and open hostility between the two powers actually to occur;—here first, we must bring before us the state of the case. Of course we must recollect, on the one hand, that Catholics are not only bound to allegiance to the British Crown, but have special privileges as citizens, can meet together, speak and pass resolutions, can vote for members of Parliament, and sit in Parliament, and can hold office, all which are denied to foreigners sojourning among us; while on the other hand there is the authority of the Pope, which, though not "absolute" even in religious matters, as Mr. Gladstone would have it to be, has a call, a supreme call on our obedience. Certainly in the event of such a collision of jurisdictions, there are cases in which we should obey the Pope and disobey the State. Suppose, for instance, an Act was passed in Parliament, bidding Catholics to attend Protestant service every week, and the Pope distinctly told us not to do so, for it was to violate our duty to our faith :—I should obey the Pope and not the Law. It will be said by Mr. Gladstone, that such a case is impossible. I know it is ; but why ask me for what I should do in extreme and utterly improbable cases such as this, if my answer cannot help bearing the character of an axiom ? It is not my fault that I must deal in truisms. The circumferences of State jurisdiction and of Papal are for the most part quite apart from each other ; there are just some few degrees out of the 360 in which they intersect, and Mr. Gladstone, instead of letting these cases of intersection alone, till they occur actually, asks me what I should do, if I found myself placed in the space intersected. If I must answer then, I should say distinctly that did the State tell me in a question of worship to do what the Pope told me not to do, I should obey the Pope, and should think it no sin, if I used all the power and the influence I possessed as a citizen to prevent such a Bill passing the Legislature, and to effect its repeal if it did.

But now, on the other hand, could the case ever occur, in which I should act with the Civil Power, and not with the Pope ? Now, here again, when I begin to imagine instances, Catholics will cry out (as Mr. Gladstone in the case I supposed, cried out in the interest of the other side), that instances never can occur. I know they cannot ; I know the Pope never can do what I am going to suppose ; but then, since it cannot possibly happen in fact, there is no harm in just saying what I should (hypothetically) do, if it did happen. I say then in certain (impossible) cases I should side, not with the Pope, but with the Civil Power. For instance, I believe members of Parliament, or of the Privy Council, take an oath that they would not acknowledge the right of succession of a Prince of Wales, if he became a Catholic. I should not consider the Pope could release me from that oath had I bound myself by it. Of course, I might exert myself to the utmost to get the act repealed which bound me; again, if I could not, I might retire from Parliament or office, and so rid myself of the engagement I had made; but I should be clear that, though the Pope bade all Catholics to stand firm in one phalanx for the Catholic Succession, still, while I remained in my office, or in my place in Parliament, I could not do as he bade me.

Again, were I actually a soldier or sailor in her Majesty's service, and sent to take part in a war which I could not in my conscience see to be unjust, and should the Pope suddenly bid all Catholic soldiers and sailors to retire from the service, here again, taking the advice of others, as best I could, I should not obey him.

What is the use of forming impossible cases? One can find plenty of them in books of casuistry, with the answers attached in respect to them. In an actual case, a Catholic would, of course, not act simply on his own judgment; at the same time, there are supposable cases in which he would be obliged to go by it solely—viz., when his conscience could not be reconciled to any of the courses of action proposed to him by others.

In support of what I have been saying, I refer to one or two weighty authorities :—

Cardinal Turrecremata says :—" Although it clearly follows from the circumstance that the Pope can err at times, and command things which must not be done, that we are not to be simply obedient to him in all things, that does not show that he must not be obeyed by all when his commands are good. To know in what cases he is to be obeyed and in what not . . it is said in the Acts of the Apostles, ' One ought to obey God rather than man ;" therefore, were the Pope to command anything against· Holy Scripture, or the articles of faith, or the truth of the Sacraments, or the commands of the natural or divine law, *he ought not to be obeyed*, but in such commands to be passed over (despiciendus)," *Summ. de Eccl.*, pp. 47, 8.

Bellarmine, speaking of resisting the Pope, says :—

" In order to resist and defend oneself no authority is required. . . Therefore, as it is lawful to resist the Pope, if he assaulted a man's person, so it is lawful to resist him, if he assaulted souls, or *troubled the state* (turbanti rempublicam), and much more if he strove to destroy the Church. It is lawful, I say, to resist him, by not doing what he commands, and hindering the execution of his will," *de Rom. Pont.*, ii. 29.

Archbishop Kenrick says :—" His power was given for edification, not for destruction. If he uses it from the love of domination (quod absit) *scarcely will he meet with obedient populations.*"—*Theol. Moral, t.* i., p. 158.

When, then, Mr. Gladstone asks Catholics how they can obey the Queen and yet obey the Pope, since it may happen that the commands of the two authorities may clash, I answer, that it is my *rule*, both to obey the one and to obey the other, but that there is no rule in this world without exceptions, and if either the Pope or the Queen demanded of me an " Absolute Obedience," he or she would be transgressing the laws of human nature and human society. I give an absolute obedience to neither. Further, if ever this double allegiance pulled me in contrary ways, which in this age of the world I think it never will, then I should decide according to the particular case, which is beyond all rule, and must be decided on its own merits. I should look to see what theologians could do for me, what the Bishops and clergy around me, what my confessor ; what friends whom I revered : and if, after all, I could not take their view of the matter, then I must rule myself by my own judgment and my own conscience. But all this is hypothetical and unreal.

Here, of course, it will be objected to me, that I am, after all, having recourse to the Protestant doctrine of Private Judgment ; not so ; it is the Protestant doctrine that Private Judgment is our *ordinary* guide in religious matters, but I use it, in the case in question, in very extraordinary and rare, nay, impossible emergencies. Do not the highest Tories thus defend the substitution of William for James II. ? It is a great mistake to suppose our state in the

Catholic Church is so entirely subjected to rule and system, that we are never thrown upon what is called by divines "the Providence of God." The teaching and assistance of the Church does not supply all conceivable needs, but those which are ordinary; thus, for instance, the sacraments are necessary for dying in the grace of God and hope of heaven, yet, when they cannot be got, acts of faith, hope, and contrition, with the desire for those aids which the dying man has not, will convey in substance what those aids ordinarily convey. And so a Catechumen, not yet baptised, may be saved by his purpose and preparation to receive the rite. And so, again, though "Out of the Church there is no salvation," this does not hold in the case of good men who are in invincible ignorance. And so it is also in the case of our ordinations; Chillingworth and Macaulay say that it is morally impossible that we should have kept up for 1800 years an Apostolical succession of ministers without some separation of the chain; and we in answer say that, however true this may be humanly speaking, there has been a special Providence over the Church to secure it. Once more, how else could private Catholics save their souls when there was a Pope and Anti-popes, each severally claiming their allegiance?

§ 5. Conscience.

It seems, then, that there are extreme cases in which Conscience may come into collision with the word of a Pope, and is to be followed in spite of that word. Now I wish to place this proposition on a broader basis, acknowledged by all Catholics, and, in order to do this satisfactorily, as I began with the prophecies of Scripture and the primitive Church, when I spoke of the Pope's prerogatives, so now I must begin with the Creator and His creature, when I would draw out the prerogatives and the supreme authority of Conscience.

I say, then, that the Supreme Being is of a certain character, which, expressed in human language, we call ethical. He has the attributes of justice, truth, wisdom, sanctity, benevolence and mercy, as eternal characteristics in His Nature, the very Law of His being, identical with Himself; and next, when He became Creator, He implanted this Law, which is Himself, in the intelligence of all His rational creatures. The Divine Law, then, is the rule of ethical truth, the standard of right and wrong, a sovereign, irreversible, absolute authority in the presence of men and Angels. "The eternal law," says St. Augustine, "is the Divine Reason or Will of God, commanding the observance, forbidding the disturbance, of the natural order of things." "The natural law," says St. Thomas, "is an impression of the Divine Light in us, a participation of the eternal law in the rational creature." (Gousset, *Theol. Moral.* t. 1, pp. 24, &c.) This law, as apprehended in the minds of individual men, is called "conscience;" and, though it may suffer refraction in passing into the intellectual medium of each, it is not thereby so affected as to lose its character of being the Divine Law, but still has, as such, the prerogative of commanding obedience. "The Divine Law," says Cardinal Gousset, "is the supreme rule

of actions; our thoughts, desires, words, acts, all that
man is, is subject to the domain of the law of God; and
this law is the rule of our conduct by means of our conscience. Hence it is never lawful to go against our conscience; as the fourth Lateran council says, 'Quidquid fit
contra conscientiam, ædificat ad gehennam.'"

This, I know, is very different from the view ordinarily
taken of it, both by the science and literature, and by the
public opinion, of this day. It is founded on the doctrine
that conscience is the voice of God, whereas it is fashion-
able on all hands now to consider it in one way or another
a creation of man. Of course, there are great and broad
exceptions to this statement. It is not true of many or
most religious bodies of men; especially not of their
teachers and ministers. When Anglicans, Wesleyans, the
various Presbyterian sects in Scotland, and other denominations among us, speak of conscience, they mean what we
mean, the voice of God in the nature and heart of man,
as distinct from the voice of Revelation. They speak of a
principle planted within us, before we have had any training,
though such training and experience is necessary for its
strength, growth, and due formation. They consider it a
constituent element of the mind, as our perception of other
ideas may be, as our powers of reasoning, as our sense of
order and the beautiful, and our other intellectual endowments. They consider it, as Catholics consider it, to be
the internal witness of both the existence and the law of
God. They think it holds of God, and not of man, as an
Angel walking on the earth would be no citizen or depen-
dent of the Civil Power. They would not allow, any more
than we do, that it could be resolved into any combination
of principles in our nature, more elementary than itself;
nay, though it may be called, and is, a law of the mind,
they would not grant that it was nothing more; I mean,
that it was not a dictate, nor conveyed the notion of responsibility, of duty, of a threat and a promise, with a vivid-
ness which discriminated it from all other constituents of
our nature.

This, at least, is how I read the doctrine of Protestants

as well as of Catholics. The rule and measure of duty is not utility, nor expedience, nor the happiness of the greatest number, nor State convenience, nor fitness, order, and the *pulchrum*. Conscience is not a long-sighted selfishness, nor a desire to be consistent with oneself; but it is a messenger from Him, who, both in nature and in grace, speaks to us behind a veil, and teaches and rules us by His representatives. Conscience is the aboriginal Vicar of Christ, a prophet in its informations, a monarch in its peremptoriness, a priest in its blessings and anathemas, and, even though the eternal priesthood throughout the Church could cease to be, in it the sacerdotal principle would remain and would have a sway.

Words such as these are idle empty verbiage to the great world of philosophy now. All through my day there has been a resolute warfare, I had almost said conspiracy, against the rights of conscience, as I have described it. Literature and science have been embodied in great institutions in order to put it down. Noble buildings have been reared as fortresses against that spiritual, invisible influence which is too subtle for science and too profound for literature. Chairs in Universities have been made the seats of an antagonist tradition. Public writers, day after day, have indoctrinated the minds of innumerable readers with theories subversive of its claims. As in Roman times, and in the middle age, its supremacy was assailed by the arm of physical force, so now the intellect is put in operation to sap the foundations of a power which the sword could not destroy. We are told that conscience is but a twist in primitive and untutored man; that its dictate is an imagination; that the very notion of guiltiness, which that dictate enforces, is simply irrational, for how can there possibly be freedom of will, how can there be consequent responsibility, in that infinite eternal network of cause and effect, in which we helplessly lie? and what retribution have we to fear, when we have had no real choice to do good or evil?

So much for philosophers; now let us see what is the notion of conscience in this day in the popular mind.

There, no more than in the intellectual world, does "conscience" retain the old, true, Catholic meaning of the word. There too the idea, the presence, of a Moral Governor is far away from the use of it, frequent and emphatic as that use of it is. When men advocate the rights of conscience, they in no sense mean the rights of the Creator, nor the duty to Him, in thought and deed, of the creature; but the right of thinking, speaking, writing, and acting, according to their judgment or their humour, without any thought of God at all. They do not even pretend to go by any moral rule, but they demand, what they think is an Englishman's prerogative, to be his own master in all things, and to profess what he pleases, asking no one's leave, and accounting priest or preacher, speaker or writer, unutterably impertinent, who dares to say a word against his going to perdition, if he like it, in his own way. Conscience has rights because it has duties; but in this age, with a large portion of the public, it is the very right and freedom of conscience to dispense with conscience, to ignore a Lawgiver and Judge, to be independent of unseen obligations. It becomes a license to take up any or no religion, to take up this or that and let it go again, to go to Church, to go to chapel, to boast of being above all religions and to be an impartial critic of each of them. Conscience is a stern monitor, but in this century it has been superseded by a counterfeit, which the eighteen centuries prior to it never heard of, and could not have mistaken for it, if they had. It is the right of self-will.

And now I shall turn aside for a moment to show how it is that the Popes of our century have been misunderstood by English people, as if they really were speaking against conscience in the true sense of the word, when in fact they were speaking against it in the various false senses, philosophical or popular, which in this day are put upon the word. The present Pope, in his Encyclical of 1864, *Quantâ curâ*, speaks, (as will come before us in the next section,) against "liberty of conscience," and he refers to his predecessor, Gregory XVI., who, in his *Mirari vos*, calls it a "deliramentum." It is a rule in formal ecclesias-

tical proceedings, as I shall have occasion to notice lower
down, when books or authors are condemned, to use the
very words of the book or author, and to condemn the
words in that particular sense which they have in their
context and their drift, not in the literal, not in the religious sense, such as the Pope might recognize, were they in
another book or author.   To take a familiar parallel, among
many which occur daily.   Protestants speak of the " Blessed
Reformation ;" Catholics too talk of " the Reformation,"
though they do not call it blessed.   Yet every " reformation " ought, from the very meaning of the word, to be good,
not bad ; so that Catholics seem to be implying a eulogy on
an event which, at the same time, they consider a surpassing
evil.   Here then they are taking the word and using it in
the popular sense of it, not in the Catholic.   They would
say, if they expressed their full meaning, " the *so-called*
reformation."   In like manner, if the Pope condemned
"the Reformation," it would be utterly sophistical to say
in consequence that he had declared himself against all
reforms ; yet this is how Mr. Gladstone treats him, because
he speaks of (so-called) liberty of conscience.   To make
this distinction clear, viz., between the Catholic sense of
the word " conscience," and that sense in which the Pope condemns it, we find in the *Recueil des Allocutions*, &c., the
words accompanied with quotation-marks, both in Pope
Gregory's and Pope Pius's Encyclicals, thus :—Gregory's,
" Ex hoc putidissimo 'indifferentismi' fonte," (mind, " indifferentismi' is under quotation-marks, because the Pope
will not make himself answerable for so unclassical a word)
" absurda illa fluit ac erronea sententia, seu potius deliramentum, asserendam esse ac vindicandam cuilibet 'libertatem conscientiæ.'"   And that of Pius, "haud timent
erroneam illam fovere opinionem a Gregorio XVI. deliramentum appellatam, nimirum 'libertatem conscientiæ' esse
proprium cujuscunque hominis jus."   Both Popes certainly scoff at the "so-called liberty of conscience," but
there is no scoffing of any Pope, in formal documents
addressed to the faithful at large, at that most serious
doctrine, the right and the duty of following that Divine

Authority, the voice of conscience, on which in truth the Church herself is built.

So indeed it is; did the Pope speak against Conscience in the true sense of the word, he would commit a suicidal act. He would be cutting the ground from under his feet. His very mission is to proclaim the moral law, and to protect and strengthen that "Light which enlighteneth every man that cometh into the world." On the law of conscience and its sacredness are founded both his authority in theory and his power in fact. Whether this or that particular Pope in this bad world always kept this great truth in view in all he did, it is for history to tell. I am considering here the Papacy in its office and its duties, and in reference to those who acknowledge its claims. They are not bound by a Pope's personal character or private acts, but by his formal teaching. Thus viewing his position, we shall find that it is by the universal sense of right and wrong, the consciousness of transgression, the pangs of guilt, and the dread of retribution, as first principles, deeply lodged in the hearts of men, thus and only thus, that he has gained his footing in the world and achieved his success. It is his claim to come from the Divine Lawgiver, in order to elicit, protect, and enforce those truths which the Lawgiver has sown in our very nature—it is this and this only—that is the explanation of his length of life more than antediluvian. The championship of the Moral Law and of conscience is his *raison d'être*. The fact of his mission is the answer to the complaints of those who feel the insufficiency of the natural light; and the insufficiency of that light is the justification of his mission.

All sciences, except the science of Religion, have their certainty in themselves; as far as they are sciences, they consist of necessary conclusions from undeniable premisses, or of phenomena manipulated into general truths by an irresistible induction. But the sense of right and wrong, which is the first element in religion, is so delicate, so fitful, so easily puzzled, obscured, perverted, so subtle in its argumentative methods, so impressible by education, so biassed by pride and passion, so unsteady in its flight, that, in the struggle for existence amid various exercises and triumphs of the human intellect, this sense is at once the highest of all teachers, yet the least luminous; and the Church, the Pope, the Hierarchy are, in the Divine purpose, the supply of an urgent demand. Natural Religion, certain as are its grounds and its doctrines as addressed to thoughtful, serious minds, needs, in order that it may speak to mankind with effect and subdue the world, to be sustained and completed by Revelation.

In saying all this, of course I must not be supposed to be limiting the Revelation of which the Church is the keeper to a mere republication of the Natural Law; but still it is true, that, though Revelation is so distinct from the teaching of nature and beyond it, yet it is not independent of it, nor without relations towards it, but is its complement, re-assertion, issue, embodiment, and interpretation. The Pope, who comes of Revelation, has no jurisdiction over Nature. If, under the plea of his revealed prerogatives, he neglected his mission of preaching truth, justice, mercy, and peace, much more, if he trampled on the consciences of his subjects,—if he had done so all along, as Protestants say, then he could not have lasted all these many centuries till now, so as to be made the mark of their reprobation. Dean Milman has told us above, how faithful he was to his duty in the medieval time, and how successful. Afterwards, for a while the Papal chair was filled by men, who gave themselves up to luxury, security, and a Pagan kind of Christianity; and we all know what a moral earthquake was the consequence, and how the Church lost, thereby, and has lost to this day, one-half of Europe. The Popes could not have recovered from so terrible a catastrophe, as they have done, had they not returned to their first and better ways, and the grave lesson of the past is in itself the guarantee of the future.

Such is the relation of the ecclesiastical power to the human conscience :—however, another view may be taken of it. It may be said that no one doubts that the Pope's power rests on those weaknesses of human nature, that religious sense, which in ancient days Lucretius noted as

the cause of the worst ills of our race ; that he uses it dex-
terously, forming under shelter of it a false code of morals
for his own aggrandisement and tyranny; and that thus
conscience becomes his creature and his slave, doing, as if
on a divine sanction, his will; so that in the abstract indeed and in idea it is free, but never free in fact, never
able to take a flight of its own, independent of him, any
more than birds whose wings are clipped ;—moreover, that,
if it were able to exert a will of its own, then there would
ensue a collision more unmanageable than that between
the Church and the State, as being in one and the same
subject matter—viz., religion; for what would become of
the Pope's " absolute authority," as Mr. Gladstone calls it, if
the private conscience had an absolute authority also ?

I wish to answer this important objection distinctly.

1. First, I am using the word " conscience " in the high
sense in which I have already explained it ; not as a fancy
or an opinion, but as a dutiful obedience to what claims
to be a divine voice, speaking within us.

2. Secondly I observe that conscience is not a judgment upon any speculative truth, any abstract doctrine, but
bears immediately on conduct, on something to be done or
not done. " Conscience," says St. Thomas, " is the practical
judgment or dictate of reason, by which we judge what *hic
et nunc* is to be done as being good, or to be avoided as
evil." Hence conscience cannot come into direct collision with
the Church's or the Pope's infallibility ; which is engaged
only on general propositions, or the condemnation of propositions simply particular.

3. Next, I observe that, conscience being a practical dictate, a collision is possible between it and the Pope's
authority only when the Pope legislates, or gives particular orders, and the like. But a Pope is not infallible
in his laws, nor in his commands, nor in his acts of state,
nor in his administration, nor in his public policy. Let it
be observed that the Vatican Council has left him just as it
found him here. Mr. Gladstone's language on this point is to
me quite unintelligible. Why, instead of using vague terms,
does he not point out precisely the very words by

which the Council has made the Pope in his acts infallible?
Instead of so doing, he assumes a conclusion which is altogether false. He says, p. 34, "First comes the Pope's
infallibility;" then in the next page he insinuates that,
under his infallibility, come acts of excommunication, as if
the Pope could not make mistakes in this field of action.
He says, p. 35, "It may be sought to plead that the Pope
does not propose to invade the country, to seize Woolwich,
or burn Portsmouth. He will only, at the worst, excommunicate opponents. . . Is this a good answer? After
all, even in the Middle Ages, it was not by the direct
action of fleets and armies of their own that the Popes
contended with kings who were refractory; it was mainly by
interdicts," &c. What have excommunication and interdict
to do with Infallibility? Was St. Peter infallible on that
occasion at Antioch when St. Paul withstood him? was St.
Victor infallible when he separated from his communion
the Asiatic Churches? or Liberius when in like manner he
excommunicated Athanasius? And, to come to later times,
was Gregory XIII., when he had a medal struck in honour
of the Bartholomew massacre? or Paul IV. in his conduct
towards Elizabeth? or Sextus V. when he blessed the
Armada? or Urban VIII. when he persecuted Galileo?
No Catholic ever pretends that these Popes were infallible
in these acts. Since then infallibility alone could block the
exercise of conscience, and the Pope is not infallible in
that subject-matter in which conscience is of supreme
authority, no dead-lock, such as is implied in the objection
which I am answering, can take place between conscience
and the Pope.

4. But, of course, I have to say again, lest I should
be misunderstood, that when I speak of Conscience, I mean
conscience truly so called. When it has the right of opposing the supreme, though not infallible Authority of the
Pope, it must be something more than that miserable counterfeit which, as I have said above, now goes by the name.
If in a particular case it is to be taken as a sacred and
sovereign monitor, its dictate, in order to prevail against
the voice of the Pope, must follow upon serious thought,

prayer, and all available means of arriving at a right judgment on the matter in question. And further, obedience to the Pope is what is called "in possession;" that is, the *onus probandi* of establishing a case against him lies, as in all cases of exception, on the side of conscience. Unless a man is able to say to himself, as in the Presence of God, that he must not, and dare not, act upon the Papal injunction, he is bound to obey it, and would commit a great sin in disobeying it. *Primâ facie* it is his bounden duty, even from a sentiment of loyalty, to believe the Pope right and to act accordingly. He must vanquish that mean, ungenerous, selfish, vulgar spirit of his nature, which, at the very first rumour of a command, places itself in opposition to the Superior who gives it, asks itself whether he is not exceeding his right, and rejoices, in a moral and practical matter, to commence with scepticism. He must have no wilful determination to exercise a right of thinking, saying, doing just what he pleases, the question of truth and falsehood, right and wrong, the duty if possible of obedience, the love of speaking as his Head speaks, and of standing in all cases on his Head's side, being simply discarded. If this necessary rule were observed, collisions between the Pope's authority and the authority of conscience would be very rare. On the other hand, in the fact that, after all, in extraordinary cases, the conscience of each individual is free, we have a safeguard and security, were security necessary (which is a most gratuitous supposition), that no Pope ever will be able, as the objection supposes, to create a false conscience for his own ends.

Now, I shall end this part of the subject, for I have not done with it altogether, by appealing to various of our theologians in evidence that, in what I have been saying, I have not misrepresented Catholic doctrine on these important points.

That is, on the duty of obeying our conscience at all hazards.

I have already quoted the words which Cardinal Gousset has adduced from the Fourth Lateran; that "He who acts against his conscience loses his soul." This *dictum* is brought out with singular fulness and force in the moral treatises of theologians. The celebrated school, known as the Salmanticenses, or Carmelites of Salamanca, lays down the broad proposition, that conscience is ever to be obeyed whether it tells truly or erroneously, and that, whether the error is the fault of the person thus erring or not.* They say that this opinion is certain, and refer, as agreeing with them, to St. Thomas, St. Bonaventura, Caietan, Vasquez, Durandus, Navarrus, Corduba, Layman, Escobar, and fourteen others. Two of them even say this opinion is *de fide*. Of course, if he is culpable in being in error, which he would have escaped, had he been more in earnest, for that error he is answerable to God, but still he must act according to that error, while he is in it, because he in full sincerity thinks the error to be truth.

Thus, if the Pope told the English Bishops to order their priests to stir themselves energetically in favour of tee-totalism, and a particular priest was fully persuaded that abstinence from wine, &c., was practically a Gnostic error, and therefore felt he could not so exert himself without sin; or suppose there was a Papal order to hold lotteries in each mission for some religious object, and a priest could say in God's sight that he believed lotteries to be morally wrong, that priest in either of these cases would commit a sin *hic et nunc* if he obeyed the Pope, whether he was right or wrong in his opinion, and, if wrong, although he had not taken proper pains to get at the truth of the matter.

Busenbaum, of the Society of Jesus, whose work I have already had occasion to notice, writes thus :—"A heretic, as long as he judges his sect to be more or equally deserving of belief, has no obligation to believe [in the Church.]" And he continues, "When men who

* " Aliqui opinantur quod conscientia erronea non obligat; Secundam sententiam, et certam, asserentem esse peccatum discordare à conscientiâ erroneâ, invincibili aut vincibili, tenet D. Thomas; quem sequuntur omnes Scholastici."—*Theol. Moral.* t. v., p. 12, ed. 1728.

E

have been brought up in heresy, are persuaded from boy-
hood that we impugn and attack the word of God, that
we are idolators, pestilent deceivers, and therefore are to be
shunned as pestilences, they cannot, while this persuasion
lasts, with a safe conscience, hear us."—t. 1, p. 54.

Antonio Corduba, a Spanish Franciscan, states the doctrine with still more point, because he makes mention of
Superiors. " In no manner is it lawful to act against conscience, even though a Law, or a Superior commands it."
—*De Conscient.*, p. 138.

And the French Dominican, Natalis Alexander:—" If,
in the judgment of conscience, though a mistaken conscience, a man is persuaded that what his Superior commands is displeasing to God, he is bound not to obey."
—*Theol.* t. 2, p. 32.

The word " Superior " certainly includes the Pope ;
but, to bring out this point clearly, Cardinal Jacobatius in
his authoritative work on Councils, which is contained in
Labbe's Collection of them, introduces the Pope by name :
—" If it were doubtful," he says, " whether a precept [of
the Pope] be a sin or not, we must determine thus :—that,
if he to whom the precept is addressed has a conscientious
sense that it is a sin and injustice, first it is his duty to
put off that sense ; but, if he cannot, nor conform himself
to the judgment of the Pope, in that case it is his duty to
follow his own private conscience, and patiently to bear it,
if the Pope punishes him."—*lib.* iv., p. 241.

Would it not be well for Mr. Gladstone to bring passages from our recognized authors as confirmatory of his
view of our teaching, as those which I have quoted are
destructive of it ? and they must be passages declaring, not
only that the Pope is ever to be obeyed, but that there are
no exceptions to the rule, for exceptions must be in all
concrete matters.

I add one remark. Certainly, if I am obliged to bring
religion into after-dinner toasts, (which indeed does not
seem quite the thing) I shall drink,—to the Pope, if you
please,—still, to Conscience first, and to the Pope afterwards.

§ 6. The Encyclical of 1864.

The subject of Conscience leads us to the Encyclical, which is one of the special objects of Mr. Gladstone's attack ; and to do justice to it, I must, as in other sections, begin from an earlier date than 1864.

Modern Rome then is not the only place where the traditions of the old Empire, its principles, provisions, and practices, have been held in honour ; they have been retained, they have been maintained in substance, as the basis of European civilization down to this day, and notably among ourselves. In the Anglican establishment the king took the place of the Pope ; but the Pope's principles kept possession. When the Pope was ignored, the relations between Pope and king were ignored too, and therefore we had nothing to do any more with the old Imperial laws which shaped those relations ; but the old idea of a Christian Polity was still in force. It was a first principle with England that there was one true religion, that it was inherited from an earlier time, that it came of direct Revelation, that it was to be supported to the disadvantage, to say the least, of other religions, of private judgment, of personal conscience. The Puritans held these principles as firmly as the school of Laud. As to the Scotch Presbyterians, we read enough about them in the pages of Mr. Buckle. The Stuarts went, but still their principles suffered no dethronement ; their action was restrained, but they were still in force, when this century opened.

It is curious to see how strikingly in this matter the proverb has been fulfilled, " Out of sight, out of mind." Men of the present generation, born in the new civilization, are shocked to witness in the abiding Papal system the words, ways, and works of their grandfathers. In my own lifetime has that old world been alive, and has gone its way. Who will say that the plea of conscience was as effectual,

sixty years ago, as it is now in England, for the toleration
of every sort of fancy religion ?   Had the Press always that
wonderful elbow-room which it has now ?   Might public
gatherings be held, and speeches made, and republicanism
avowed in the time of the Regency, as is possible now ?
Were the thoroughfares open to monster processions at that
date, and the squares and parks at the mercy of Sunday
manifestations ?   Could *savants* in that day insinuate what
their hearers mistook for atheism in scientific assemblies,
and artizans practise it in the centres of political action ?
Could public prints day after day, or week after week, carry
on a war against religion, natural and revealed, as now is
the case ?   No ; law or public opinion would not suffer it ;
we may be wiser or better now, but we were then in the
wake of the Holy Roman Church, and had been so from the
time of the Reformation.   We were faithful to the tradition
of fifteen hundred years.   All this was called Toryism, and
men gloried in the name ; now it is called Popery and
reviled.

　　When I was young the State had a conscience, and the
Chief Justice of the day pronounced, not as a point of obsolete law, but as an energetic, living truth, that Christianity
was the law of the land.   And by Christianity was meant
pretty much what Bentham calls Church-of-Englandism, its
cry being the dinner toast, " Church and king." Blackstone,
though he wrote a hundred years ago, was held, I believe,
as an authority, on the state of the law in this matter, up to
the beginning of this century.   On the supremacy of Religion he writes as follows, that is, as I have abridged him for
my purpose.

　　" The belief of a future state of rewards and punishments,
&c., &c.,...these are the grand foundation of all judicial
oaths.   All moral evidence, all confidence in human veracity,
must be weakened by irreligion, and overthrown by infidelity.
Wherefore all affronts to Christianity, or endeavours to
depreciate its efficacy, are highly deserving of human punishment.   It was enacted by the statute of William III. that if
any person *educated in*, and *having made profession of*, the
Christian religion, shall by writing, printing, teaching, or

advised speaking, deny the Christian religion to be true, or the Holy Scriptures to be of divine authority," or again in like manner, " if any person *educated* in the Christian religion shall by writing, &c., deny any one' of the Persons of the Holy Trinity to be God, or maintain that there are more gods than one, he shall on the first offence be rendered incapable to hold any office or place of trust ; and for the second, be rendered incapable of bringing any action, being guardian, executor, legatee, or purchaser of lands, and shall suffer three years' imprisonment without bail. To give room, however, for repentance, if, within four months after the first conviction, the delinquent will in open court publicly renounce his error, he is discharged for that once from all disabilities."

Again : "those who absent themselves from the divine worship in the established Church, through total irreligion, and attend the service of no other persuasion, forfeit one shilling to the poor every Lord's day they so absent themselves, and £20 to the king, if they continue such a default for a month together. And if they keep any inmate, thus irreligiously disposed, in their houses, they forfeit £10 per month."

Further, he lays down that "reviling the ordinances of the Church is a crime of a much grosser nature than the other of non-conformity ; since it carries with it the utmost indecency, arrogance, and ingratitude ;—indecency, by setting up private judgment in opposition to public ; arrogance, by treating with contempt and rudeness what has at least a better chance to be right than the singular notions of any particular man ; and ingratitude, by denying that indulgence and liberty of conscience to the members of the national Church, which the retainers to every petty conventicle enjoy."

Once more : " In order to secure the established Church against perils from non-conformists of all denominations, infidels, Turks, Jews, heretics, papists, and sectaries, there are two bulwarks erected, called the Corporation and Test Acts ; by the former, no person can be legally elected to any office relating to the government of any city or corpo-

ration, unless, within a twelvemonth before, he has received
the sacrament of the Lord's Supper according to the rites
of the Church of England ;.........the other, called the Test
Act, directs all officers, civil and military, to make the
declaration against transubstantiation within six months
after their admission, and also within the same time to
receive the sacrament according to the usage of the Church
of England." The same test being undergone by all persons
who desired to be naturalized, the Jews also were excluded
from the privileges of Protestant churchmen.

Laws, such as these, of course gave a tone to society, to
all classes, high and low, and to the publications, periodical
or other, which represented public opinion. Dr. Watson, who
was the liberal prelate of his day, in his answer to Paine,
calls him (unless my memory betrays me) " a child of the
devil and an enemy of all righteousness." Cumberland, a
man of the world, (here again I must trust to the memory
of many past years) reproaches a Jewish writer for ingratitude in assailing, as he seems to have done, a tolerant religious establishment ; and Gibbon, an unbeliever, feels himself at liberty to look down on Priestly, whose " Socinian
shield," he says, " has been repeatedly pierced by the mighty
spear of Horsley, and whose trumpet of sedition may at
length awake the magistrates of a free country."

Such was the position of free opinion and dissenting
worship in England till quite a recent era, when one after
another the various disabilities which I have been recount-
ing, and many others besides, melted away, like snow at
spring-tide ; and we all wonder how they could ever have
been in force. The cause of this great revolution is obvious, and its effect inevitable. Though I profess to be an
admirer of the principles now superseded, in themselves,
mixed up as they were with the imperfections and· evils
incident to everything human, nevertheless I say frankly
I do not see how they could possibly be maintained in the
ascendant. When the intellect is cultivated, it is as certain
that it will develop into a thousand various shapes, as that
infinite hues and tints and shades of colour will be reflected
from the earth's surface, when the sun-light touches it ;

and in matters of religion the more, by reason of the extreme subtlety and abstruseness of the mental action by
which they are determined. During the last seventy years,
first one class of the community, then another, has awakened
up to thought and opinion. Their multiform views on
sacred subjects necessarily affected and found expression in
the governing order. The State in past time had a conscience ; George the Third had a conscience ; but there
were other men at the head of affairs besides him with consciences, and they spoke for others besides themselves, and
what was to be done, if he could not work without them,
and they could not work with him, as far as religious questions came up at the Council-board ? This brought on a
dead-lock in the time of his successor. The ministry of the day
could not agree together in the policy or justice of keeping up
the state of things which Blackstone describes.   The State
ought to have a conscience ; but what if it happen to have
half-a-dozen, or a score, or a hundred, in religious matters,
each different from each ?   I think Mr. Gladstone has
brought out the difficulties of the situation himself
in his Autobiography. No government could be formed,
if religious unanimity was a *sine qua non.* What
then was to be done ? As a necessary consequence,
the whole theory of Toryism, hitherto acted on, came
to pieces and went the way of all flesh. This was in
the nature of things. Not a hundred Popes could have
hindered it, unless Providence interposed by an effusion of
divine grace on the hearts of men, which would amount to
a miracle, and perhaps would interfere with human responsibility. The Pope has denounced the sentiment that he
ought to come to terms with " progress, liberalism, and
the new civilization." I have no thought at all of disputing his words. I leave the great problem to the future.
God will guide other Popes to act when Pius goes, as He
has guided him. No one can dislike the democratic principle more than I do. No one mourns, for instance, more
than I, over the state of Oxford, given up, alas ! to
" liberalism and progress," to the forfeiture of her great medieval motto, " Dominus illuminatio mea," and with a consequent

call on her to go to Parliament or the Heralds College for a new one ; but what can we do ? All I know is, that Tory-ism, that is, loyalty to persons, " springs immortal in the human breast;" that Religion is a spiritual loyalty ; and that Catholicity is the only divine form of Religion. And thus, in centuries to come, there may be found out some way of uniting what is free in the new structure of society with what is authoritative in the old, without any base compromise with " Progress" and " Liberalism."

But to return :—I have noticed the great revolution in the state of the Law which has taken place since 1828 for this reason :—to suggest that Englishmen, who within fifty years kept up the Pope's system, are not exactly the par-ties to throw stones at the Pope for keeping it up still.

But I go further :—in fact the Pope has not said on this subject of conscience (for that is the main subject in question) what Mr. Gladstone, makes him say. On this point I desiderate that fairness in his Pamphlet which we have a right to expect from him ; and in truth his unfair-ness is wonderful. He says, pp. 15, 16, that the Holy See has " condemned " the maintainers of " the Liberty of the Press, of conscience, and of worship." Again, that the " Pontiff has condemned free speech, free writing, a free press, toleration of non-conformity, liberty of conscience," p. 42. Now, is not this accusation of a very wholesale character ? Who would not understand it to mean that the Pope had pronounced a universal anathema against all these liberties in toto, and that English law, on the contrary, allowed those liberties in toto, which the Pope had condemned. But the Pope has done no such thing. The real question is in what respect, in what measure, has he spoken against liberty : the grant of liberty admits of de-grees. Blackstone is careful to show how much more liberty the law allowed to the subject in his day, how much less severe it was in its safeguards against abuse, than it had used to be ; but he never pretends that it is conceivable that liberty should have no boundary at all. The very idea of political society is based upon the principle that each member of it gives up a portion of his natural liberty for advantages which are greater than that liberty ; and the question is, whether the Pope, in any act of his which touches us Catholics, in any ecclesiastical or theological statement of his, has propounded any principle, doctrine, or view, which is not carried out in fact at this time in British courts of law, and would not be conceded by Blackstone.   I repeat, the very notion of human society is a relinquishment, to a certain point, of the liberty of its members individually, for the sake of a common security.   Would it be fair on that account to say that the British Constitution condemns *all* liberty of con- science in word and in deed ?

We Catholics, on our part, are denied liberty of our religion by English law in various ways, but we do not complain, because a limit must be put to even innocent liberties, and we acquiesce in it for the social compen- sations which we gain on the whole.   Our school boys cannot play cricket on Sunday, not even in country places, for fear of being taken before a magistrate and fined.   In Scotland we cannot play the piano on Sundays, much less the fiddle, even in our own rooms.   I have had before now a lawyer's authority for saying that a religious procession is illegal even within our own premises.   Till the last year or two we could not call our Bishops by the titles which our Religion gave them.   A mandate from the Home Secretary obliged us to put off our cassocks when we went out of doors.   We are forced to pay rates for the establish- ment of secular schools which we cannot use, and then we have to find means over again for building schools of our own.   Why is not all this as much an outrage on our con- science as the prohibition upon Protestants at Rome, Naples, and Malaga, before the late political changes—not to hold their services in a private, or in the ambassador's house, or outside the walls,—but to flaunt them in public and thereby to irritate the natives ?   Mr. Gladstone seems to think it is monstrous for the Holy See to sanction such a prohibition.   If so, may we not call upon him to gain for us in Birmingham " the free exercise of our religion," in making a circuit of the streets in our vestments, and chanting the " Pange Lingua," and the protection of the police against the mob which would be sure to gather round us, —particularly since we are English born ; but the Protestants at Malaga or Naples were foreigners.* But we have the good sense neither to feel it a hardship, nor to protest against it as a grievance.

But now for the present state of English Law :—I say seriously Mr. Gladstone's accusation of us avails quite as much against Blackstone's four volumes, against laws in general, against the social contract, as against the Pope. What the Pope has said, I will show presently : first let us see what the statute book has to tell us about the present state of English liberty of speech, of the press, and of worship.

First, as to public speaking and meetings :—do we allow of seditious language, or of insult to the sovereign, or his representatives ? Blackstone says, that a misprision is committed against him by speaking or writing against him, cursing or wishing him ill, giving out scandalous stories concerning him, or doing anything that may tend to lessen him in the esteem of his subjects, may weaken his government, or may raise jealousies between him and his people." Also he says, that " threatening and reproachful words to any judge sitting in the Courts " involve " a high misprision, and have been punished with large fines, imprisonment, and corporal punishment." And we may recollect quite lately the judges of the Queen's Bench prohibited public meetings and speeches which had for their object the issue of a case then proceeding in Court.

Then, again, as to the Press, there are two modes of bridling it, one before the printed matter is published, the other after. The former is the method of censorship, the latter that of the law of libel. Each is a restriction on the liberty of the Press. We prefer the latter. I never heard it said that the law of libel was of a mild character ; and I never heard that the Pope, in any Brief or Rescript, had insisted on a censorship.

* " Hominibus illuc immigrantibus." These words Mr. Gladstone omits, also he translates " publicum" "free," pp. 17, 18.

Lastly, liberty of worship : as to the English restriction of it, we have had a notable example of it in the last session of Parliament, and we shall have still more edifying illustrations of it in the next, though not certainly from Mr. Gladstone. The ritualistic party, in the free exercise of their rights, under the shelter of the Anglican rubrics, of certain of the Anglican offices, of the teaching of their great divines, and of their conscientious interpretation of their Articles, have, at their own expense, built churches for worship after their own way ; and, on the other hand, Parliament and the newspapers are attempting to put them down, not so much because they are acting against the tradition and the law of the Establishment, but because of the national dislike and dread of the principles and doctrines which their worship embodies.

When Mr. Gladstone has a right to say broadly, by reason of these restrictions, that British law and the British people condemn the maintainers of liberty of conscience, of the press, and of worship, *in toto*, then may he say so of the Encyclical, or account of those words which to him have so frightful a meaning.

Now then let us see, on the other hand, what the proposition is, the condemnation of which leads him to say, that the Pope has unrestrictedly " condemned those who maintain *the* liberty of the Press, *the* liberty of conscience and of worship, and *the* liberty of speech," p. 16,—has " condemned. free speech, free writing, and a free press," p. 42. The condemned proposition speaks as follows :—

" Liberty of conscience and worship, is the *inherent right* of all men. 2. It ought to be proclaimed in *every* rightly constituted society. 3. It is a right to *all sorts of liberty* (omnimodam libertatem) such, that it ought not to be restrained by any authority, ecclesiastical *or civil*, as far as public speaking, printing, or any other public manifestation of opinions is concerned."

Now, is there any government on earth that could stand the strain of such a doctrine as this ? It starts by taking for granted that there are certain Rights of man ; Mr. Gladstone so considers, I believe ; but other deep thinkers of the day are quite of another opinion ; however, if the doctrine of the proposition is true, then the right of conscience, of which it speaks, being inherent in man, is of universal force—that is, all over the world—also, says the proposition, it is a right which must be recognized by all rightly constituted governments. Lastly, what is the right of conscience thus inherent in our nature, thus necessary for all states? The proposition tells us. It is the liberty of *every* one to give *public* utterance, in *every* possible shape, by *every* possible channel, without *any* let or hindrance from God or man, to *all* his notions *whatsoever*.*

Which of the two in this matter is peremptory and sweeping in his utterance, the author of this thesis himself, or the Pope who has condemned what he has uttered? Who is it who would force upon the world a universal? All that the Pope has done is to deny a universal, and what a universal! a universal liberty to all men to say out whatever doctrines they may hold by preaching, or by the press, uncurbed by church or civil power. Does not this bear out what I said in the foregoing section of the sense in which Pope Gregory denied a "liberty of conscience?" It is a liberty of self-will. What if a man's conscience embraces the duty of regicide? or infanticide? or free love? You may say that in England the good sense of the nation would stifle and extinguish such atrocities. True, but the proposition says that it is the very right of every one, by nature, in every well constituted society. If so, why have we gagged the Press in Ireland on the ground of its being seditious? Why is not India brought within the British constitution? It seems a light epithet for the Pope to use, when he calls such a doctrine of conscience *deliramentum* : of all conceivable absurdities it is the wildest and most stupid. Has Mr.

* "Jus civibus *inesse* ad *omnimodam* libertatem, *nullâ* vel ecclesiasticâ vel civili auctoritate coarctandam, quo suos conceptus *quoscunque* sive voce, sive typis, sive aliâ ratione, *palam publiceque* manifestare ac declarare valeant."

Gladstone really no better complaint to make against the Pope's condemnations than this?

Perhaps he will say, Why should the Pope take the trouble to condemn what is so wild? But he does : and to say that he condemns something which he does not condemn, and then to inveigh against him on the ground of that something else, is neither just nor logical.

●

§ 7. THE SYLLABUS.

NOW I come to the Syllabus of " Errors," the publication of which has been exclaimed against in England as
such singular enormity, and especially by Mr. Gladstone.
The condemnation of theological statements which militate
against the Catholic Faith is of long usage in the Church.
Such was the condemnation of the heresies of Wickliffe in
the Council of Constance ; such those of Huss, of Luther,
of Baius, of Jansenius ; such the condemna⁺ions which
were published by Sextus IV., Innocent XI., Clement XI.,
Benedict XIV., and other Popes. Such condemnations
are no invention of Pius IX. The Syllabus is a collection of such erroneous propositions, as he has condemned during his Pontificate ; there are 80 of them.

The word "Syllabus" means a collection ; the French
translation calls it a " *Resumé* ;"—a Collection of what ?
I have already said, of propositions,—propositions which the
Pope in his various Allocutions, Encyclicals, and like documents, since he has been Pope, has pronounced to be
Errors. Who gathered the propositions out of these Papal
documents, and put them together in one ? We do not
know ; all we know is that, by the Pope's command, this
Collection of Errors was sent by his Foreign Minister to
the Bishops. He, Cardinal Antonelli, sent to them at the
same time the Encyclical of December, 1864, which is a
document of dogmatic authority. The Cardinal says, in
his circular to them, that the Pope ordered him to do so.
The Pope thought, he says, that perhaps the Bishops had
not seen some of his Allocutions, and other authoritative
letters and speeches of past years ; in consequence the Pope
had had the Errors which, at one time or other he had
therein condemned, brought together into one, and that for
the use of the Bishops.

Such is the Syllabus and its object. There is not a word

in it of the Pope's own writing ; there is nothing in it at all but the Erroneous Propositions themselves—that is, except the heading " A Syllabus, containing the principal Errors of our times, which are noted in the Consistorial Allocutions, in the Encyclicals, and in other Apostolical Letters of our most Holy Lord, Pope Pius IX." There is one other addition—viz., after each proposition a reference is given to the Allocution, Encyclical, or other document in which it is condemned.

The Syllabus, then, is to be received with profound submission, as having been sent by the Pope's authority to the Bishops of the world. It certainly has indirectly his extrinsic sanction; but intrinsically, and viewed in itself, it is nothing more than a digest of certain Errors made by an anonymous writer. There would be nothing on the face of it, to show that the Pope had ever seen it, page by page, unless the " Imprimatur " implied in the Cardinal's letter had been an evidence of this. It has no mark or seal put upon it which gives it a direct relation to the Pope. Who is its author ? Some select theologian or high official doubtless ; can it be Cardinal Antonelli himself ? No surely : any how it is not the Pope, and I do not see my way to accept it for what it is not. I do not speak as if I had any difficulty in recognizing and condemning the Errors which it catalogues, did the Pope himself bid me ; but he has not as yet done so, and he cannot delegate his *Magisterium* to another. I wish with St. Jerome to " speak with the Successor of the Fisherman and the Disciple of the Cross." I assent to that which the Pope propounds in faith and morals, but it must be he speaking officially, personally, and immediately, and not any one else, who has a hold over me. The Syllabus is not an official act, because it is not signed, for instance, with " Datum Romæ, Pius P. P. IX," or " sub annulo Piscatoris," or in some other way; it is not a personal, for he does not address his " Venerabiles Fratres," or " Dilecto Filio," or speak as " Pius Episcopus ;" it is not an immediate, for it comes to the Bishops only through the Cardinal Minister of State.

If, indeed, the Pope should ever make that anonymous

compilation directly his own, then of course I should bow to it and accept it as strictly His. He might have done so; he might do so still; again, he might issue a fresh list of Propositions in addition, and pronounce them to be Errors, and I should take that condemnation to be of dogmatic authority, because I believe him appointed by his Divine Master to determine in the detail of faith and morals what is true and what is false. But such an act of his he would formally authenticate; he would speak in his own name, as Leo X. or Innocent XI. did, by Bull or Letter Apostolic. Or, if he wished to speak less authoritatively, he would speak through a Sacred Congregation; but the Syllabus makes no claim to be acknowledged as the word of the Pope. Moreover, if the Pope drew up that catalogue, as it may be called, he would discriminate the errors one from another, for they greatly differ in gravity, and he would guard against seeming to say that all intellectual faults are equal. What gives cogency to this remark is, that a certain number of Bishops and theologians, when a Syllabus was in contemplation, did wish for such a formal act on the part of the Pope, and in consequence they drew up for his consideration the sort of document on which, if he so willed, he might suitably stamp his infallible sanction; but he did not accede to their prayer. This composition is contained iu the " *Recueil des Allocutions,*" &c., and is far more than a mere " collection of errors." It is headed, " Theses ad Apostolicam Sedem delatæ *cum censuris,*" &c., and each error from first to last has the ground of its condemnation marked upon it. There are sixty-one of them. The first is " impia, injuriosa religioni," &c.; the second is " complexivè sumpta, falsa," &c.; the third the same; the fourth " hæretica," and so on, the epithets affixed having a distinct meaning, and denoting various degrees of error. Such a document, unlike the Syllabus, has a substantive character.

Here I am led to interpose a remark;—it is plain, then, that there are those near, or with access, to the Holy Father, who would, if they could, go much further in the way of assertion and command, than the divine *Assistentia,* which overshadows him, wills or permits : so that his acts and his words on doctrinal subjects must be carefully scrutinized and weighed, before we can be sure what really he has said. Utterances which must be received as coming from an Infallible Voice are not made every day, indeed they are very rare ; and those which are by some persons affirmed or assumed to be such, do not always turn out what they are said to be ; nay, even such as are really dogmatic must be read by definite rules and by traditional principles of interpretation, which are as cogent and unchangeable as the Pope's own decisions themselves. What I have to say presently will illustrate this truth ; meanwhile I use the circumstance which has led to my mentioning it, for another purpose here. When intelligence which we receive from Rome startles and pains us from its seemingly harsh or extreme character, let us learn to have some little faith and patience, and not take for granted that all that is reported is the truth. There are those who wish and try to carry measures, and declare they have carried, when they have not carried them. How many strong things, for instance, have been reported with a sort of triumph on one side and with irritation and despondency on the other, of what the Vatican Council has done ; whereas the very next year after it, Bishop Fessler, the Secretary General of the Council, brings out his work on " True and False Infallibility,"* reducing what was said to be so monstrous to its true dimensions. When I see all this going on, those grand lines always rise on my lips in the Greek Tragedy—

" Οὔποτε τὰν Διὸς ἁρμονίαν
θνατῶν παρεξίασι βουλαί,"—

and still more the consolation given us by a Divine Speaker that, though the swelling sea is so threatening to look at, yet there is One who rules it and says, " Hitherto shalt thou come and no further, and here shall thy proud waves be stayed !"

But to return :—the Syllabus then has no dogmatic force ; it addresses us, not in its separate portions, but as a whole,

---

* A translation of this important work will in a few days be published by Messrs. Burns and Oates.

and is to be received from the Pope by an act of obedience, not of faith, that obedience being shown by having recourse to the original and authoritative documents, (Allocutions and the like,) to which the Syllabus pointedly refers. Moreover, when we turn to those documents, which *are* authoritative, we find the Syllabus cannot even be called an echo of the Apostolic Voice ; for, in matters in which wording is so important, it is not an exact transcript of the words of the Pope, in its account of the errors condemned,—just as would be natural in what is an index for reference.

Mr. Gladstone indeed wishes to unite the Syllabus to that Encyclical which so moved him in December, 1864, and says that the Errors noted in the Syllabus are all brought under the infallible judgment pronounced on certain errors specified in the Encyclical. This is an untenable assertion. He says of the Pope and of the Syllabus, p. 20 : "These are not mere opinions of the Pope himself, nor even are they opinions which he might paternally recommend to the pious consideration of the faithful. With the promulgation of his opinions is unhappily combined, in the Encyclical Letter *which virtually, though not expressly, includes the whole,* a *command* to all his spiritual children (from which command we, the disobedient children, are in no way excluded) *to hold them,*" and he appeals in proof of this to the language of the Encyclical ; but let us see what that language is. The Pope speaks thus, as Mr. Gladstone himself quotes him : " All and each of the wrong opinions and doctrines, *mentioned one by one in this Encyclical (hisce litteris)*, by our Apostolical authority, we reprobate, &c." He says, as plainly as words can speak, that the wrong opinions which in this passage he condemns, are specified *in* the Encyclical, not outside of it ; and, when we look into the earlier part of it, there they are, about ten of them ; there is not a single word in the Encyclical to show that the Pope in it was alluding to the Syllabus. The Syllabus does not exist as far as the language of the Encyclical is concerned. This' gratuitous assumption seems to me marvellously unfair.

The only connexion between the Syllabus and the Encyclical is one external to them both, the connexion of time and organ ; Cardinal Antonelli sending them both to the Bishops with the introduction of one and the same letter. In that letter he speaks to the Bishops thus, as I paraphrase his words :*—The Holy Father sends you by me a list, which he has caused to be drawn up and printed, of the errors which he has in various formal documents, in the course of the last eighteen years, condemned. At the same time, and with that list of errors, he is sending you a new Encyclical, which he has judged it *apropos* to write to the Catholic Bishops ;—so I send you both at once."

The Syllabus, then, is a list, or rather an index, of the Pope's Encyclical or Allocutional condemnations, an index *raisonné*,—not alphabetical, as is found, for instance, in Bellarmine's or Lambertini's works,—drawn up by the Pope's orders, out of his paternal care for the flock of Christ, and conveyed to the Bishops through his Minister of State. But we can no more accept it as *de fide*, as a dogmatic document, than other index or table of contents. Take a parallel case, *mutatis mutandis* : Counsel's opinion being asked on a point of law, he goes to his law books, writes down his answer, and, as authority, refers his client to 23 George III., c. 5, s. 11 ; 11 Victoria, c. 12, s. 19, and to Thomas *v.* Smith, Att.-Gen. *v.* Roberts, and Jones *v.* Owen. Who would say that that sheet of foolscap had force of law, when it was nothing more than a list of references to the Statutes of the Realm, or Judges' decisions, in which the Law's voice really was found ?

The value of the Syllabus, then, lies in its references ; but of these Mr. Gladstone has certainly availed himself very little. Yet, in order to see the nature and extent of

---

* His actual words (abridged) are these :—"Notre T.S.S. Pius IX. n'a jamais cessé de proscrire les principales erreurs de notre très-malheureuse époque, par ses Encycliques, et par ses Allocutions, &c. Mais, comme il peut arriver que tous les actes pontificaux ne perviennent pas a chacun des Ordinaires, le même Souverain Pontife a voulu que l'on rédigeât un Syllabus de ces mêmes erreurs, destiné à être envoyé à tous les Evêques, &c. Il m'a ensuite ordonné de veiller à ce que ce Syllabus imprimé fût envoyé a V.E.R. dans ce temps où le même Souverain Pontife a jugé à propos d'écrire un autre Lettre Encyclique. Ainsi, je m'empresse d'envoyer a V.E. ce Syllabus avec ces Lettres."

the condemnation passed on any proposition of the Syllabus, it is absolutely necessary to turn out the passage of the Allocution, Encyclical, or other document, in which the condemnation is found ; for the wording of the errors which the Syllabus contains is to be interpreted by its reierences. Instead of this Mr. Gladstone uses forms of speech about the Syllabus which only excite in me fresh wonder. Indeed, he speaks upon these ecclesiastical subjects generally in a style in which priests and parsons are accused by their enemies of speaking concerning geology. For instance, the Syllabus, as we have seen, is a list or index ; but he calls it " extraordinary declarations," p. 21. How can a list of Errors be a series of Pontifical " Declarations ?"

However, perhaps he would say that, in speaking of " Declarations," he was referring to the authoritative statements which I have accused him of neglecting. With all my heart ; but then let us see how those statements fulfil the character he gives of them. He calls them " Extraordinary declarations on personal and private duty," p. 21, and "stringent condemnations," p. 19. Now, I certainly must grant that some are stringent, but only some. One of the most severe that I have found among them is that in the Apostolic Letter of June 10, 1851, against some heretic priest out at Lima, whose elaborate work in six volumes against the Curia Romana, is pronounced to be in its various statements scandalous, rash, false, schismatical, injurious to the Roman Pontiffs and Ecumenical Councils impious and heretical." It well deserved to be called by these names, which are not terms of abuse, but each with its definite meaning ; and, if Mr Gladstone, in speaking of the condemnations, had confined his epithet " stringent" to it, no one would have complained of him. And another severe condemnation is that of the works of Professor Nuytz. But let us turn to some other of the so-called condemnations, in order to ascertain whether they answer to his general description of them.

1. For instance, take his own 16th (the 77th of the " erroneous Propositions ") that, " It is no longer expedient

that the Catholic Religion should be established to the exclusion of all others." When we turn to the Allocution, which is the ground of its being put into the Syllabus, what do we find there? First, that the Pope was speaking, not of States universally, but of one particular State, Spain, definitely Spain; secondly, he was not speaking of the proposition in question directly, or dogmatically, or separately, but was protesting against the breach in many ways of the Concordat on the part of the Spanish government; further, that he was not referring to any theological work containing it, nor contemplating any proposition; nor, on the other hand, using . any word of condemnation at all, nor using any harsher terms of the Government in question than those of "his wonder and bitterness." And again, taking the Pope's remonstrance as it stands, is it any great cause of complaint to Englishmen, who so lately were severe in their legislation upon Unitarians, Catholics, unbelievers and others, that the Pope does merely *not* think it expedient for *every* state *from this time forth* to tolerate *every* sort of religion on its territory, and to disestablish the Church at once? for this is all that he denies. As in the instance in the foregoing section, he does but deny a universal, which the "erroneous proposition" asserts without any explanation.

2. Another of Mr. Gladstone's "stringent Condemnations" (his 18th) is that of the Pope's denial of the proposition that "the Roman Pontiff can and ought to come to terms with Progress, Liberalism, and the New Civilization." I turn to the Allocution of March 18, 1861, and find there no formal condemnation of this Proposition at all. The Allocution is a long *argument* to the effect that the moving parties in that Progress, Liberalism, and new Civilization, make use of it so seriously to the injury of the Faith and the Church, that it is both out of the power, and contrary to the duty, of the Pope to come to terms with them. Nor would those prime movers themselves differ from him here; certainly in this country it is the common cry that Liberalism is and will be the Pope's destruction, and they wish and mean it so to be. This Allocution on the subject is at once beautiful, dignified,

and touching: and I cannot conceive how Mr. Gladstone should make stringency his one characteristic of these condemnations, especially when after all there is here no condemnation at all.

3. Take, again, Mr. Gladstone's 15th—" That the abolition of Temporal Power of the Popedom would be highly advantageous to the Church." Neither can I find in the Pope's Allocution any formal condemnation whatever of this proposition, much less a " stringent " one. Even the Syllabus does no more in the case of any one of the eighty, than to call it an " error ;" and what the Pope himself says of this particular error is only this :—" We cannot but in particular *warn* and *reprove* (monere et redarguere) those who applaud the decree by which the Roman Pontiff has been despoiled of all the honour and dignity of his civil rule, and assert that the said decree, more than anything else, conduces to the liberty and prosperity of the Church itself."—*Alloc.*, April 20, 1849..

4. Take another of his instances, the 17th, the " error " that "in countries called Catholic the public exercise of other religions may laudably be allowed." I have had occasion to mention already his mode of handling the Latin text of this proposition—viz., that, whereas the men who were forbidden the public exercise of their religion were foreigners, who had no right to be in a country not their own at all, and might fairly have conditions imposed upon them during their stay there ; nevertheless Mr. Gladstone (apparently through haste) has left out the word " hominibus illuc immigrantibus," on which so much turns. Next, as I have observed above, it was only the sufferance of their public worship, and again of all worships whatsoever, however many and various, which the Pope blamed ; further, the the Pope's words did not apply to all States, but specially, and, as far as the Allocution goes, definitely, to New Granada.

However, the point I wish to insist upon here is, that there was in this case no condemned proposition at all, but it was merely, as in the case of Spain, an act of the Government which the Pope protested against. The Pope merely told that Government that that act, and other acts which they had committed, gave him very great pain ; that he had expected better things of them ; that the way they went on was all of a piece; and they had his best prayers. Somehow, it seems to me strange, for any one to call an expostulation like this one of a set of "extraordinary declarations" "stringent condemnations."

I am convinced that the more the propositions and the references contained in the Syllabus are examined, the more signally will the charge break down, brought against the Pope on occasion of it : as to those Propositions which Mr. Gladstone specially selects, some of them I have already taken in hand, and but few of them present any difficulty.

5. As to those on Marriage, I cannot follow Mr. Gladstone's meaning here, which seems to me very confused, and it would be going out of the line of remark which I have traced out for myself, (and which already is more extended than I could wish), were I to treat of them.

6. His fourth Error, (taken from the Encyclical) that "Papal judgments and decrees may, without sin, be disobeyed or differed from," is a denial of the principle of Hooker's celebrated work on Ecclesiastical Polity, and would be condemned by him as well as by the Pope. And it is plain to common sense that no society can stand if its rules are disobeyed. What club or union would not expel members who refused so to be bound ?

7. And the 5th,* 8th, and 9th propositions are necessarily errors, if the Sketch of Church Polity drawn out in former sections is true, and are necessarily considered as such by those, as the Pope, who maintain that Polity.

8. The 10th Error, as others which I have noticed above, is a *universal* (that "in the conflict of laws, civil and ecclesiastical, the civil law should prevail"), and the Pope does but deny a universal.

* Father Coleridge, in his Sermon on "The Abomination of Desolation," observes that, whereas Proposition 5th speaks of "jura," Mr. Gladstone translates "*civil* jura." Vid. that Sermon, and the "Month" for December, for remarks on various of these Propositions ; but above all Mgr. Dupanloup's works on the subject, Messrs. Burns and Oates, 1865.

9. Mr. Gladstone's 11th, which I do not quite understand in his wording of it, runs thus :—" Catholics can
approve of that system of education for youth which is separated from the Catholic faith and the Church's power, and
which regards the science only of physical things, and the
outlines (fines) of earthly social life alone or at least primarily." How is this not an "Error?" Surely there are
Englishmen enough who protest against the elimination
of religion from our schools ; is such a protest so dire an
offence to Mr. Gladstone ?

10. And the 12th Error is this :—That " the science of
philosophy and of morals, also the laws of the State, can
and should keep clear of divine and ecclesiastical authority." This too will not be anything short of an error in
the judgment of great numbers of our own people.   Is
Benthamism so absolutely the Truth, that the Pope is to be
denounced because he has not yet become a convert to it ?

11. There are only two of the condemnations which
really require a word of explanation ; I have already
referred to them. One is that of Mr. Gladstone's sixth
Proposition, "Roman Pontiffs and Ecumenical Councils,
have departed from the limits of their power, have usurped
the rights of Princes, and even in defining matters of
faith and morals have erred." These words are taken
from the Lima Priest's book.   We have to see then what
he means by " the Rights of Princes," for the proposition is condemned in *his* sense of the word.   It is
a rule of the Church in the condemnation of a book to
state the proposition condemned in the words of the book
itself, without the Church being answerable for the words
employed.*   I have already referred to this rule in my

* Propositiones, de quibus Ecclesia judicium suum pronunciat, duobus
præsertim modis spectari possunt, vel absolute ac in se ipsis, vel relativè ad
sensum libri et auctoris.   In censurâ propositionis alicujus auctoris vel
libri, Ecclesia attendit ad sensum ab eo intentum, qui quidem ex verbis,
ex totâ doctrinæ ipsius serie, libri textura et confirmatione, consilio, in-
stitutoque elicitur.   Propositio libri vel auctoris *æquivoca* esse potest, dupli-
cemque habere sensum, rectum unum et alterum malum.   *Ubi còntingit
Ecclesiam propositiones hujusmodi æquivocas absque præviâ distinctione
sensuum configere, censura unicè cadit in sensum perversum libri vel auctoris.*—Tournely t. 2, p. 170, ed. 1752.

5th section. Now · this Priest included among the rights of Catholic princes that of deposing Bishops from their sacred Ministry, of determining the impediments to marriage, of forming Episcopal sees, and of being free from episcopal authority in spiritual matters. When, then, the Proposition is condemned "that Popes had usurped the rights of Princes;" what is meant is, "the so-called rights of Princes," which were really the rights of the Church, in assuming which there was no usurpation at all.

12. The other proposition, Mr. Gladstone's seventh, the condemnation of which requires a remark, is this: "The Church has not the power to employ force (vis inferendæ) nor any temporal power direct or indirect." This is one of a series of Propositions found in the work of Professor Nuytz, entitled, "Juris Ecclesiastici Institutiones," all of which are condemned in the Pope's Apostolic Letter of August 22, 1851. Now here " employing force " is not the Pope's phrase but Professor Nuytz's, and the condemnation is meant to run thus, " It is an error to say, with Professor Nuytz, that what *he* calls 'employing force' is not allowable to the Church." That this is the right interpretation of the " error " depends of course on a knowledge of the Professor's work, which I have never had an opportunity of seeing; but here I will set down what the received doctrine of the Church is on ecclesiastical punishments, as stated in a work of the highest authority, since it comes to us with letters of approval from Gregory XVI. and Pius IX.

"The opinion," says Cardinal Soglia, " that the coercive power divinely bestowed upon the Church consists in the infliction of spiritual punishments alone, and not in corporal or temporal, seems more in harmony with the gentleness of the Church. Accordingly I follow their judgment, who withdraw from the Church the corporal sword, by which the body is destroyed or blood is shed. Pope Nicholas thus writes : 'The Church has no sword but the spiritual. She does not kill, but gives life, hence that well-known saying, ' Ecclesia abhorret a sanguine.' But the lighter

punishments, though temporal and corporal, such as shut-
ting up in a monastery, prison, flogging, and others of the
same kind, short of effusion of blood, the Church *jure suo*
can inflict."—(Institut. Jur., pp. 161, 9, Paris.)

And the Cardinal quotes the words of Fleury, "The
Church has enjoined on penitent sinners almsgivings,
fastings, and other corporal inflictions. . . Augustine
speaks of beating with sticks, as sanctioned by the Bishops,
after the manner of masters in the case of servants, par-
ents in the case of children and schoolmasters of scholars.
Abbots flogged monks in the way of paternal and domestic
chastisement .. Imprisonment for a set time or for life is
mentioned among canonical penances; priests and other
clerics, who had been deposed for their crimes, being
committed to prison in order that they might pass the
time to come in penance for their crime, which thereby
was withdrawn from the memory of the public."

But now I have to answer one question. If what I
have said is substantially the right explanation to give to
the drift and contents of the Syllabus, have not I to account
for its making so much noise, and giving such deep and wide
offence on its appearance? It has already been reprobated
by the voice of the world. Is there not, then, some reason
at the bottom of the aversion felt by educated Europe
towards it, which I have not mentioned? This is a very
large question to entertain, too large for this place; but
I will say one word upon it.

Doubtless one of the reasons of the excitement and displeasure which the Syllabus caused and causes so widely,
is the number and variety of the propositions marked as
errors, and the systematic arrangement to which they were
subjected. So large and elaborate a work struck the public
mind as a new law, moral, social and ecclesiastical, which
was to be the foundation of a European code, and the
beginning of a new world, in opposition to the social principles of the 19th century; and there certainly were persons in high station who encouraged this idea. When
this belief was once received, it became the interpretation

of the whole Syllabus through the eighty Propositions, of which it recorded the erroneousness; as if they were all portions of one great scheme of aggression. Then, when the public was definitively directed to the examination of these *Theses damnatæ*, their drift and the meaning of their condemnation was sure to be misunderstood, from the ignorance, in the case of all but ecclesiastics, of the nature and force of ecclesiastical language. The condemnations had been published in the Pope's Encyclicals and Allocutions in the course of the preceding eighteen years, and no one had taken any notice of them; now, when they were brought all together, they on that very account made a great sensation. Next, that same fact seemed in itself a justification, with minds already prejudiced, for expecting in each of them something extraordinary, and even hostile, to society; and then, again, when they were examined one by one, certainly their real sense was often not obvious, and could not be, to the intelligence of laymen, high and low, educated and simple.

Another circumstance, which I am not theologian enough to account for, is this,—that the wording of many of the erroneous propositions, as they are drawn up in the Syllabus, gives an apparent breadth to the matter condemned which is not found in the Pope's own words in his Allocutions and Encyclicals. Not that really there is any difference between the Pope's words and Cardinal Antonelli's, for (as I have shown in various instances) what the former says in the concrete, the latter does but repeat in the abstract; or, to speak logically when the Pope enunciates as true the particular affirmative, "New Granada ought to keep up the establishment of the Catholic Religion," then (since its contradictory is necessarily false) the Cardinal declares," "To say that no State should keep up the establishment of the Catholic Religion is an error." But there is a dignity and beauty in the Pope's own language which the Cardinal's abstract Syllabus cannot have, and this gave to opponents an opportunity to declaim against the Pope, which opportunity was in no sense afforded by what he said himself.

Then, again, it must be recollected, in connexion with what I have said, that theology is a science, and a science of a special kind; its reasoning, its method, its modes of expression, and its language are all its own. Every science must be in the hands of a comparatively few persons—that is, of those who have made it a study. The courts of law have a great number of rules in good measure traditional; so has the House of Commons, and, judging by what one reads in the public prints, men must have a noviceship there before they can be at perfect ease in their position. In like manner young theologians, and still more those who are none, are sure to mistake in matters of detail; indeed a really first-rate theologian is rarely to be found. At Rome the rules of interpreting authoritative documents are known with a perfection which at this time is scarcely to be found elsewhere. Some of these rules, indeed, are known to all priests; but even this general knowledge is not possessed by laymen, much less by Protestants, however able and experienced in their own several lines of study or profession. One of those rules I have had several times occasion to mention. In the censure of books, which offend against doctrine or discipline, it is a common rule to take sentences out of them in the author's own words, whether those words are in themselves good or bad, and to affix some note of condemnation to them in the sense in which they occur in the book in question. Thus it may happen that even what seems at first sight a true statement, is condemned for being made the shelter of an error; for instance: " Faith justifies when it works," or " there is no religion where there is no charity," may be taken in a good sense; but each proposition is condemned in Quesnell, because it is false as he uses it.

A further illustration of the necessity of a scientific education in order to understand the value of Propositions, is afforded by a controversy which has lately gone on among us as to the validity of Abyssinian Orders. In reply to a document urged on one side of the question, it was allowed on the other, that, " if that document was to be read in the same way as we should read any ordinary judgment, the interpretation which had been given to it was the most obvious and natural." "But it was well known," it was said, "to those who are familiar with the practical working of such decisions, that they are only interpreted with safety in the light of certain rules, which arise out of what is called the *stylus curiæ*." And then some of these rules were given; first, "that to understand the real meaning of a decision, no matter how clearly set forth, we should know the nature of the difficulty or *dubium*, as it was understood by the tribunal that had to decide upon it. Next, nothing but the direct proposition, in its nudest and severest sense, as distinguished from indirect propositions, the grounds of the decision, or implied statements, is ruled by the judgment. Also, if there is anything in the wording of a decision which appears inconsistent with the teaching of an approved body of theologians, &c., the decision is to be interpreted so as to leave such teaching intact;" and so on.* It is plain that the view thus opened upon us has further bearings than that for which I make use of it here.

These remarks on scientific theology apply also of course to its language. I have employed myself in illustration in framing a sentence, which would be plain enough to any priest, but I think would perplex any Protestant. I hope it is not of too light a character to introduce here. We will suppose then a theologian to write as follows:— "Holding, as we do, that there is only *material* sin in those who, being *invincibly* ignorant, reject the truth, therefore in charity we hope that they have the future portion of *formal* believers, as considering that by *virtue* of their good faith, though not of the *body* of the faithful, they *implicitly* and *interpretatively* believe what they seem to deny."

What sense would this statement convey to the mind of a member of some Reformation Society or Protestant League? He would read it as follows, and consider it all

* Month, Nov. and Dec., 1873.

the more insidious and dangerous for its being so very unintelligible :—" Holding, as we do, that there is only a very considerable sin in those who reject the truth out of contumacious ignorance, therefore in charity we hope that they have the future portion of nominal Christians, as considering, that by the excellence of their living faith, though not in the number of believers, they believe without any hesitation, as interpreters |of Scripture ?] what they seem to deny."

Now, considering that the Syllabus was intended for the Bishops, who would be the interpreters of it, as the need arose, to their people, and it got bodily into English newspapers even before it was received at many an episcopal residence, we shall not be surprised at the commotion which accompanied its publication.

I have spoken of the causes intrinsic to the Syllabus, which have led to misunderstandings about it. As to external, I can be no judge myself as to what Catholics who have means of knowing are very decided in declaring, the tremendous power of the Secret Societies. It is enough to have suggested here, how a wide-spread organization like theirs might malign and frustrate the most beneficial acts of the Pope. One matter I had information of myself from Rome at the time when the Syllabus had just been published, before there was yet time to ascertain how it would be taken by the world at large. Now, the Rock of St. Peter on its summit enjoys a pure and serene atmosphere, but there is a great deal of Roman *malaria* at the foot of it. While the Holy Father was in great earnestness and charity addressing the Catholic world by his Cardinal Minister, there were circles of light-minded men in his city who were laying bets with each other whether the Syllabus would "make a row in Europe" or not. Of course it was the interest of those who betted on the affirmative side to represent the Pope's act to the greatest disadvantage ; and it was very easy to kindle a flame in the mass of English and other visitors at Rome which with a very little nursing was soon strong enough to take care of itself.

§ 8. THE VATICAN COUNCIL.

IN beginning to speak of the Vatican Council, I am obliged from circumstances to begin by speaking of myself. The most unfounded and erroneous assertions have publicly been made about my sentiments towards it, and as confidently as they are unfounded. Only a few weeks ago it was stated categorically by some anonymous correspondent of a Liverpool paper, with reference to the prospect of my undertaking the task on which I am now employed, that it was, "in fact, understood that at one time Dr. Newman was on the point of uniting with Dr. Dollinger and his party, and that it required the earnest persuasion of several members of the Roman Catholic Episcopate to prevent him from taking that step,"—an unmitigated and most ridiculous untruth in every word of it, nor would it be worth while to notice it here, except for its connexion with the subject on which I am entering.

But the explanation of such reports about me is easy. They arise from forgetfulness on the part of those who spread them, that there are two sides of ecclesiastical acts, that right ends are often prosecuted by very unworthy means, and that in consequence those who, like myself, oppose a mode of action, are not necessarily opposed to the issue for which it has been adopted. Jacob gained by wrong means his destined blessing. " All are not Israelites, who are of Israel," and there are partizans of Rome who have not the sanctity and wisdom of Rome herself.

I am not referring to anything which took place within the walls of the Council chambers ; of that of course we know nothing ; but even though things occurred there which it is not pleasant to dwell upon, that would not at all affect, not by an hair's breadth, the validity of the resulting definition, as I shall presently show. What

I felt deeply, and ever shall feel, while life lasts, is the violence and cruelty of journals and other publications, which, taking as they professed to do the Catholic side, employed themselves by their rash language (though, of course, they did not mean it so), in unsettling the weak in faith, throwing back inquirers, and shocking the Protestant mind. Nor do I speak of publications only; a feeling was too prevalent in many places that no one could be true to God and His Church, who had any pity on troubled souls, or any scruple of "scandalizing those little ones who believe in" Christ, and of "despising and destroying him for whom He died."

It was this most keen feeling, which made me say, as I did continually, "I will not believe that the Pope's Infallibility will be defined, till defined it is."

Moreover, a private letter of mine became public property. That letter, to which Mr. Gladstone has referred with a compliment to me which I have not merited, was one of the most confidential I ever wrote in my life. I wrote it to my own Bishop, under a deep sense of the responsibility I should incur, were I not to speak out to him my whole mind. I put the matter from me when I had said my say, and kept no proper copy of the letter. To my dismay I saw it in the public prints: to this day I do not know, nor suspect, how it got there. I cannot withdraw it, for I never put it forward, so it will remain on the columns of newspapers whether I will or not; but I withdraw it as far as I can, by declaring that it was never meant for the public eye.

1. So much as to my posture of mind before the Definition: now I will set down how I felt after it. On July 24, 1870, I wrote as follows :—

"I saw the new Definition yesterday, and am pleased at its moderation—that is, if the doctrine in question is to be defined at all. The terms are vague and comprehensive; and, personally, I have no difficulty in admitting it. The question is, does it come to me with the authority of an Ecumenical Council?

"Now the *primâ facie* argument is in favour of its

having that authority. The Council was legitimately called; it was more largely attended than any Council before it; and innumerable prayers from the whole of Christendom, have preceded and attended it, and merited a happy issue of its proceedings.

" Were it not then for certain circumstances, under which the Council made the definition, I should receive that definition at once. Even as it is, if I were called upon to profess it, I should be unable, considering it came from the Holy Father and the competent local authorities, at once to refuse to do so. On the other hand, it cannot be denied that there are reasons for a Catholic, till better informed, to suspend his judgment on its validity.

" We all know that ever since the opening of the Council, there has been a strenuous opposition to the definition of the doctrine; and that, at the time when it was actually passed, more than eighty Fathers absented themselves from the Council, and would have nothing to do with its act. But, if the fact be so, that the Fathers were not unanimous, is the definition valid ? This depends on the question whether unanimity, at least moral, is or is not necessary for its validity ? As at present advised I think it is; certainly Pius IV. lays great stress on the unanimity of the Fathers in the Council of Trent. ' Quibus rebus perfectis,' he says in his Bull of Promulgation, ' concilium tantâ *omnium qui illi interfuerunt* concordiâ peractum fuit, ut consensum plane *a Domino* effectum esse constiterit; idque in nostris atque omnium oculis valdè mirabile fuerit.'

" Far different has been the case now,—though the Council is not yet finished. But, if I must now at once decide what to think of it, I should consider that all turned on what the dissentient Bishops now do.

" If they separate and go home without acting as a body, if they act only individually, or as individuals, and each in his own way, then I should not recognize in their opposition to the majority that force, firmness, and unity of view, which creates a real case of want of moral unanimity in the Council.

" Again, if the Council continues to sit, if the dissentient Bishops more or less take part in it, and concur in its acts ; if there is a new Pope, and he continues the policy of the present ; and if the Council terminates without any reversal or modification of the definition, or any effective movement against it on the part of the dissentients, then again there will be good reason for saying that the want of a moral unanimity has not been made out.

" And further, if the definition is consistently received by the whole body of the faithful, as valid, or as the expression of a truth, then too it will claim our assent by the force of the great dictum, 'Securus judicat orbis terrarum.'

"This indeed is a broad principle by which all acts of the rulers of the Church are ratified.   But for it, we might reasonably question some of the past Councils or their acts."

Also I wrote as follows to a friend, who was troubled at the way in which the dogma was passed, in order to place before him in various points of view the duty of receiving it :—

"July 27, 1870.

" I have been thinking over the subject which just now gives you and me with thousands of others, who care for religion, so much concern.

" First, till better advised, nothing shall make me say that a mere majority in a Council, as opposed to a moral unanimity, in itself creates an obligation to receive its dogmatic decrees.   This is a point of history and precedent, and of course on further examination I may find myself wrong in the view which I take of history and precedent; but I do not, cannot see, that a majority in the present Council can of itself *rule* its own sufficiency, without such external testimony.

" But there are other means by which I can be brought under the obligation of receiving a doctrine as a dogma. If I am clear that there is a primitive and uninterrupted tradition, as of the divinity of our Lord ; or where a high probability drawn from Scripture or Tradition is partially or probably confirmed by the Church. Thus a particular Catholic might be so nearly sure that the promise to Peter in Scripture proves that the infallibility of Peter is a necessary dogma, as only to be kept from holding it as such by the absence of any judgment on the part of the Church, so that the present unanimity of the Pope and 500 Bishops, even though not sufficient to constitute a formal Synodal act, would at once put him in the position, and lay him under the obligation, of receiving the doctrine as a dogma, that is, to receive it with its anathema.

"Or again, if nothing definitely sufficient from Scripture or Tradition can be brought to contradict a definition, the fact of a legitimate Superior having defined it, may be an obligation in conscience to receive it with an internal assent. For myself, ever since I was a Catholic, I have held the Pope's infallibility as a matter of theological opinion; at least, I see nothing in the Definition which necessarily contradicts Scripture, Tradition, or History; and the "Doctor Ecclesiæ," (as the Pope is styled by the Council of Florence) bids me accept it. In this case, I do not receive it on the word of the Council, but on the Pope's self-assertion.

"And I confess, the fact that all along for so many centuries the Head of the Church and Teacher of the faithful and Vicar of Christ has been allowed by God to assert virtually his infallibility, is a great argument in favour of the validity of his claim.

"Another ground for receiving the dogma, still not upon the direct authority of the Council, or with acceptance of the validity of its act *per se*, is the consideration that our Merciful Lord would not care so little for His elect people, the multitude of the faithful, as to allow their visible Head, and such a large number of Bishops to lead them into error, and an error so serious, if an error. This consideration leads me to accept the doctrine as a dogma, indirectly indeed from the Council, but not so much from a Council, as from the Pope and a very large number of Bishops. The question is not whether they had a right to impose, or even were right in imposing the dogma on the faithful; but whether, having done so, I have not an obligation to accept it, according to the maxim, 'Fieri non debuit, factum valet.'"

This letter, written before the minority had melted away, insists on this principle, that a Council's definition would have a virtual claim on our reception, even though it were not passed *conciliariter*, but in some indirect way; as, for, instance, to use a Parliamentary expression, in general committee, the great object of a Council being in some way or other to declare the judgment of the Church. I think the third Ecumenical will furnish an instance of what I mean. There the question in dispute was settled and defined, even before certain constituent portions of the Episcopal body had made their appearance; and this, with a protest of 68 of the Bishops then present against 82. When the remaining 43 arrived, these did more than protest against the definition which had been carried; they actually anathematised the Fathers who carried it, whose number seems to have stood altogether at 124 against 111; and in this state of disunion the Council ended. How then was its definition valid? By after events, which I suppose must be considered complements, and integral portions of the Council. The heads of the various parties entered into correspondence with each other, and at the end of two years their differences with each other were arranged. There are those who have no belief in the authority of Councils at all, and feel no call upon them to discriminate between one Council and another; but Anglicans, who are so fierce against the Vatican, and so respectful towards the Ephesine, should consider what good reason they have for swallowing the third Council, while they strain out the nineteenth.

The Council of Ephesus furnishes us with another remark, bearing upon the Vatican. It was natural for men who were in the minority at Ephesus to think that the faith of the Church had been brought into the utmost peril by the definition of the Council which they had unsuccessfully opposed. They had done so from their conviction that that definition gave great encouragement to religious errors in the opposite extreme to those which it condemned; and, in fact, I think that, humanly speaking, the peril was extreme. The event proved it to be so, when twenty years afterwards another Council was held under the successors of the majority at Ephesus and carried triumphantly those very errors whose eventual success had been predicted by the minority. But Providence is never wanting to His Church. St. Leo, the Pope of the day, interfered with this heretical Council, and the innovating party was stopped in its career. Its acts were cancelled at the great Council of Chalcedon, the Fourth Ecumenical, which was held under the Pope's guidance, and, without of course touching the definition of the Third, which had been settled once for all, trimmed the balance of doctrine by completing it, and excluded for ever from the Church those errors which seemed to have received some sanction at Ephesus. There is nothing of course that can be reversed in the Vatican definitions; but, should the need arise, (which is not likely,) to set right a false interpretation, another Leo will be given us for the occasion; "in monte Dominus videbit."

In this remark, made for the benefit of those who need it, as I do not myself, I shelter myself under the following passage of Molina, which a friend has pointed out to me :—
"Though the Holy Ghost has always been present to the Church, to hinder error in her definitions, and in consequence they are all most true and consistent, yet it is not therefore to be denied, that God, when any matters have to be defined, requires of the Church a co-operation and investigation of those matters, and that, in proportion to the quality of the men who meet together in Councils, to the investigation and diligence which is applied, and the greater or less experience and knowledge which is possessed more at one time than at other times, definitions more or less perspicuous are drawn up and matters are defined more exactly and completely at one time than at other times. . . . And, whereas by disputations, persevering reading, meditation, and investigation of matters, there is wont to be increased in course of time the knowledge and understanding of the same, and the Fathers of the later Councils are assisted by the investigation and definitions of the former,

hence it arises that the definitions of later Councils are wont to be more luminous, fuller, more accurate and exact than those of the earlier. Moreover, it belongs to the later Councils to interpret and to define more exactly and fully what in earlier Councils have been defined less clearly, fully, and exactly." (*De Concord. Lib. Arbit.*, &c., xiii. 15, p. 59.)

2. The other main objection to the Vatican Council is founded upon its supposed neglect of history in the decision which its Definition embodies. This objection is touched upon by Mr. Gladstone in the beginning of his Pamphlet, where he speaks of its " repudiation of ancient history," and I have an opportunity given me of noticing it here.

He asserts that, during the last forty years, " more and more have the assertions of continuous uniformity of doctrine " in the Catholic Church " receded into scarcely penetrable shadow. More and more have another series of assertions, of a living authority, ever ready to open, adopt, and shape Christian doctrine according to the times, taken their place." Accordingly, he considers that a dangerous opening has been made in the authoritative teaching of the Church for the repudiation of ancient truth and the rejection of new. However, as I understand him, he withdraws this charge from the controversy he has initiated (though not from his Pamphlet) as far as it is aimed at the pure theology of the Church. It " belongs," he says, " to the theological domain," and "is a matter unfit for him to discuss, as it is a question of divinity." It has been, then, no duty of mine to consider it, except as it relates to matters ecclesiastical ; but I am unwilling, when a charge has been made against our theology, though unsupported, yet unretracted, to leave it altogether without reply ; and that the more, because, after renouncing " questions of divinity " at p. 14, nevertheless Mr. Gladstone brings them forward again at p. 15, speaking, as he does, of the " deadly blows of 1854 and 1870 at the old, historic, scientific, and moderate school" by the definitions of the Immaculate Conception and Papal Infallibility.

Mr. Gladstone then insists on the duty of " maintaining the truth and authority of history, and the inestimable value

of the historic spirit ;" and so far of course I have the pleasure of heartily agreeing with him. As the Church is a
sacred and divine creation, so in like manner her history,
with its wonderful evolution of events, the throng of great
actors who have a part in it, and its multiform literature,
stained though its annals are with human sin and error,
and recorded on no system, and by uninspired authors, still
is a sacred work also; and those who make light of it, or
distrust its lessons, incur a grave responsibility. But it is
not every one who can read its pages rightly ; and certainly
I cannot follow Mr. Gladstone's reading of it. He is too
well informed indeed, too large in his knowledge, too acute
and comprehensive in his views, not to have an acquaintance with history far beyond the run of even highly
educated men ; still, when he accuses us of deficient attention to history, one cannot help asking, whether he does
not, as a matter of course, take for granted as true the
principles for using it familiar with Protestant divines, and
denied by our own, and in consequence whether his impeachment of us does not resolve itself into the fact that he
is Protestant and we are Catholics. Nay, has it occurred
to him that perhaps it is the fact, that we have views on
the relation of History to Dogma different from those which
Protestants maintain ? And is he so certain of the facts of
History in detail, of their relevancy, and of their drift, as
to have a right, I do not say to have an opinion of his own,
but to publish to the world, on his own warrant, that we
have "repudiated ancient history ?" He publicly charges
us, not merely with having "neglected" it, or "garbled"
its evidence, or with having contradicted certain ancient
usages or doctrines to which it bears witness, but he says
"repudiated." He could not have used a stronger term,
supposing the Vatican Council had, by a formal act, cut
itself off from early times, instead of professing, as it does
(hypocritically, if you will, but still professing) to speak
"supported by Holy Scripture and the decrees both of preceding Popes and General Councils," and "faithfully adhering
to the aboriginal tradition of the Church." Ought any one
but an *oculatus testis*, a man whose profession was to

acquaint himself with the details of history, to claim to himself the right of bringing, on his own authority, so extreme a charge against so august a power, so inflexible and rooted in its traditions through the long past, as Mr. Gladstone would admit the Roman Church to be ?

Of course I shall be reminded that, though Mr. Gladstone cannot be expected to speak on so large a department of knowledge with the confidence decorous in one who has made a personal study of it, there are others who have a right to do so ; and that by those others he is corroborated and sanctioned. There are authors, it may be said, of so commanding an authority from their learning and their honesty, that, for the purposes of discussion or of controversy, what they say may be said by any one else without presumption or risk of confutation. I will never say a word of my own against those learned and distinguished men to whom I refer. No : their present whereabout, wherever it is, is to me a thought full of melancholy. It is a tragical event, both for them and for us, that they have left us. It robs us of a great *prestige;* they have left none to take their place. I think them utterly wrong in what they have done and are doing ; and, moreover, I agree as little in their view of history as in their acts. Extensive as may be their historical knowledge, I have no reason to think that they, more than Mr. Gladstone, would accept the position which History holds among the *Loci Theologici,* as Catholic theologians determine it ; and I am denying not their report of facts, but their use of the facts they report, and that, because of that special stand-point from which they view the relations existing between the records of History and the enunciations of Popes and Councils. They seem to me to expect from History more than History can furnish, and to have too little confidence in the Divine Promise and Providence as guiding and determining those enunciations.

Why should Ecclesiastical History, any more than the text of Scripture, contain in it " the whole counsel of God ?" Why should private judgment be unlawful in interpreting Scripture against the voice of authority, and yet be lawful in the interpretation of History? There are those who make short work of questions such as these by denying authoritative interpretation altogether; that is their private concern, and no one has a right to inquire into their reason for so doing; but the case would be different were such a man to come forward publicly, and to arraign others, without first confuting their theological *præambula*, for repudiating history, or for repudiating the Bible.

For myself, I would simply confess that no doctrine of the Church can be rigorously proved by historical evidence; but at the same time that no doctrine can be simply disproved by it. Historical evidence reaches a certain way, more or less, towards a proof of the Catholic doctrines; often nearly the whole way; sometimes it goes only so far as to point in their direction; sometimes there is only an absence of evidence for a conclusion contrary to them; nay, sometimes there is an apparent leaning of the evidence to a contrary conclusion, which has to be explained;—in all cases there is a margin left for the exercise of faith in the word of the Church. He who believes the dogmas of the Church only because he has reasoned them out of History, is scarcely a Catholic. It is the Church's use of History in which the Catholic believes; and she uses other informants also, Scripture, Tradition, the ecclesiastical sense, or φρόνημα, and a subtle ratiocinative power, which in its origin is a divine gift. There is nothing of bondage or "renunciation of mental freedom" in this view, any more than in the converts of the Apostles believing what the Apostles might preach to them or teach them out of Scripture.

What has been said of History in relation to the formal Definitions of the Church, applies also to the exercises of Ratiocination. Our logical powers, too, being a gift from God, may claim to have their informations respected; and Protestants sometimes accuse our theologians, for instance, the medieval schoolmen, of having used them in divine matters a little too freely. But it has ever been our teaching and our protest that, as there are doctrines which lie beyond the direct evidence of history, so there are doctrines which transcend the discoveries of reason; and, after all, whether they are more or less recommended to us by the one informant or the other, in all cases the immediate motive in the mind of a Catholic for his reception of them is, not that they are proved to him by Reason or by History, but because Revelation has declared them by means of that high ecclesiastical *Magisterium* which is their legitimate exponent.

What has been said also applies to those other truths, with which Ratiocination has more to do than History, which are sometimes called developments of Christian doctrine, truths which are not upon the surface of the Apostolic *depositum*—that is, the legacy of Revelation,—but which from time to time are brought into form by theologians, and sometimes have been proposed to the faithful by the Church, as direct objects of faith. No Catholic would hold that they ought to be logically deduced in their fulness and exactness from the belief of the first centuries, but only this,—that, on the assumption of the Infallibility of the Church (which will overcome every objection except a contradiction in thought), there is nothing greatly to try the reason in such difficulties as occur in reconciling those evolved doctrines with the teaching of the ancient Fathers; such development being evidently the new form, explanation, transformation, or carrying out of what in substance was held from the first, what the Apostles said, but have not recorded in writing, or would necessarily have said under our circumstances, or if they had been asked, or in view of certain uprisings of error, and in that sense really portions of the legacy of truth, of which the Church, in all her members, but especially in her hierarchy, is the divinely appointed trustee.

Such an evolution of doctrine has been, as I would maintain, a law of the Church's teaching from the earliest times, and in nothing is her title of " semper eadem " more remarkably illustrated than in the correspondence of her ancient and modern exhibition of it. As to the ecclesiastical Acts of 1854 and 1870, I think with Mr. Gladstone that the principle of doctrinal development, and that of authority, have never in the proceedings of the Church been so freely and largely used as in the Definitions then promulgated to the faithful; but I deny that at either time the testimony of history was repudiated or perverted. The utmost that can be fairly said by an opponent against the theological decisions of those years is, that antecedently to the event, it might appear that there were no sufficient historical grounds in behalf of either of them—I do not mean for a personal belief in either, but—for the purpose of converting a doctrine long existing in the Church into a dogma, and making it a portion of the Catholic Creed. This adverse anticipation was proved to be a mistake by the fact of the definition being made.

3. Here I will say just a few words on the case of Pope Honorius, whose condemnation by anathema in the 6th Ecumenical Council, is certainly a strong *primâ facie* argument against the Pope's doctrinal infallibility. His case is this :—Sergius, Patriarch of Constantinople, favoured, or rather did not condemn, a doctrine concerning our Lord's Person which afterwards the sixth Council pronounced to be heresy. He consulted Pope Honorius upon the subject, who in two formal letters declared his entire concurrence with Sergius's opinion. Honorius died in peace, but, more than forty years after him, the 6th Ecumenical Council was held, which condemned him as a heretic on the score of those two letters. The simple question is, whether the heretical documents proceeded from him as an infallible authority or as a private Bishop.

Now I observe that, whereas the Vatican Council has determined that the Pope is infallible only when he speaks *ex cathedrâ*, and that, in order to speak *ex cathedrâ*, he must at least speak " as exercising the office of Pastor and Doctor of all Christians, defining, by virtue of his Apostolical authority, a doctrine whether of faith or of morals for the acceptance of the universal Church " (though Mr. Gladstone strangely says, p. 34, " There is *no* established or accepted definition of the phrase *ex cathedrâ*") from this Pontifical and dogmatic explanation of the phrase it follows, that, whatever Honorius said in answer to Sergius, and whatever he held, his words were not *ex cathedrâ*, and therefore did not proceed from his infallibility

I say so first, because he could not fulfil the above conditions of an *ex cathedrâ* utterance, if he did not actually *mean* to fulfil them. The question is unlike the question about the Sacraments ; external and positive acts, whether material actions or formal words, speak for themselves. Teaching on the other hand has no sacramental visible signs ; it is mainly a question of intention. Who would say that the architriclinus at the wedding 'feast who said, "Thou hast kept the good wine until now," was teaching the Christian world, though the words have a great ethical and evangelical sense ? What is the worth of a signature, if a man does not consider he is signing ? The Pope cannot address his people East and West, North and South, without meaning it, as if his very voice, the sounds from his lips, could literally be heard from pole to pole ; nor can he exert his " Apostolical authority " without knowing he is doing so ; nor can he draw up a form of words and use care and make an effort in doing so accurately, without intention to do so ; and, therefore, no words of Honorius proceeded from his prerogative of infallible teaching, which were not accompanied with the intention of exercising that prerogative ; and who will dream of saying, be he Anglican, Protestant, unbeliever, or on the other hand Catholic, that Honorius in the 7th century did actually intend to exert that infallible teaching voice which has been dogmatically recognized in the nineteenth ?

What resemblance do these letters of his, written almost as private instructions, bear to the "Pius Episcopus, Servus Servorum Dei, Sacro approbante Concilio, ad *perpetuam rei memoriam*," with the "Si quis huic nostræ definitioni contradicere, (quod Deus avertat), præsumpserit, *anathema* sit " of the *Pastor Æternus*? What to the "Venerabilibus fratribus, Patriarchis, primatibus, Archiepiscopis, et Episcopis *universis*," &c., and with the date and signature, " Datum Romæ apud Sanctum Petrum, Die 8 Dec. anno 1864, &c. Pius P.P. IX." of the *Quantâ curâ?*

Secondly, it is no part of our doctrine, as I shall say in my next section, that the discussions previous to a Council's definition, or to an *ex Cathedrâ* utterance of a

Pope, are infallible, and these letters of Honorius on their very face are nothing more than portions of a discussion with a view to some final decision.

For these two reasons the condemnation of Honorius by the Council in no sense compromises the doctrine of Papal Infallibility. At the utmost it only decides that Honorius in his own person was a heretic, which is inconsistent with no Catholic doctrine ; but we may rather hope and believe that the anathema fell, not upon him, but upon his letters in their objective sense, he not intending personally what his letters legitimately expressed.

4. I have one more remark to make upon the argumentative method by which the Vatican Council was carried on to its definition. The *Pastor Æternus* refers to various witnesses as contributing their evidence towards the determination of the contents of the *depositum*, such as Tradition, the Fathers and Councils, History, and especially Scripture. For instance, the Bull, speaks of the Gospel (" juxta Evangelii testimonia," c. 1) and of Scripture " manifesta S.S. Scripturarum doctrina," c. 1 : " apertis S.S. Literarum testimoniis," c. 3. " S.S. Scripturis consentanea," c. 4.) And it lays an especial stress on three passages of Scripture in particular—viz., " Thou art Peter," &c., Matthew xvi, 16-19 ; " I have prayed for thee," &c., Luke xxii., 32, and "Feed My sheep," &c., John xxi., 15-17. Now I wish all objectors to our method of reasoning from Scripture would view it in the light of the following passage in the great philosophical work of Butler, Bishop of Durham.

He writes as follows—"As it is owned the whole scheme of Scripture is not yet understood, so, if it ever comes to be understood, before the ' restitution of all things,' and without miraculous interpositions, it must be in the same way as natural knowledge is come at, by the continuance and progress of learning and of liberty, and by particular persons attending to, comparing, and pursuing intimations scattered up and down it, which are overlooked and disregarded by the generality of the world. For this is the way in which all improvements are made by thoughtful men tracing on obscure hints, as it were, dropped us by nature accidentally, or which seem to come into our minds by chance. Nor is it at all incredible that a book, which has been so long in the possession of mankind, should contain many truths as yet undiscovered. For all the same phenomena, and the same faculties of investigation, from which such great discoveries in natural knowledge have been made in the present and last age, were equally in the possession of mankind several thousand years before. And possibly it might be intended that events, as they come to pass, should open and ascertain the meaning of several parts of Scripture," ii. 3, *vide* also ii. 4, fin.

What has the long history of the contest for and against the Pope's infallibility been, but a growing insight through centuries into the meaning of those three texts, to which I just now referred, ending at length by the Church's definitive recognition of the doctrine thus gradually manifested to her?

§ 9 THE VATICAN DEFINITION.

Now I am to speak of the Vatican definition, by which the doctrine of the Pope's infallibility has become *de fide,* that is, a truth necessary to be believed, as being included in the original divine revelation, for those terms, revelation, *depositum,* dogma, and *de fide,* are correlatives ; and I begin with a remark which suggests the drift of all I have to say about it.   It is this :—that so difficult a virtue is faith, even with the special grace of God, in proportion as the reason is exercised, so difficult is it to assent inwardly to propositions, verified to us neither by reason nor experience, but depending for their reception on the word of the Church as God's oracle, that she has ever shown the utmost care to contract, as far as possible, the range of truths and the sense of propositions, of which she demands this absolute reception.   "The Church," says Pallavicini, "as far as may be, has ever abstained from imposing upon the minds of men that commandment, the most arduous of the Christian Law—viz., to believe obscure matters without doubting."*   To co-operate in this charitable duty has been one special work of her theologians, and rules are laid down by herself, by tradition, and by custom, to assist them in the task.   She only speaks when it is necessary to speak ; but hardly has she spoken out magisterially some great general principle, when she sets her theologians to work to explain her meaning in the concrete, by strict interpretation of its wording, by the illustration of its circumstances, and by the recognition of exceptions, in order to make it as tolerable as possible, and the least of a temptation, to self-willed, independent, or wrongly educated minds. A few years ago it was the fashion among us to

* Quoted by Father Ryder, (to whom I am indebted for other of my references,) in his "Idealism in Theology," p. 25.

call writers, who conformed to this rule of the Church, by the name of "Minimizers;" that day of tyrannous *ipse-dixits*, I trust, is over: Bishop Fessler, a man of high authority, for he was Secretary General of the Vatican Council, and of higher authority still in his work, for it has the approbation of the Sovereign Pontiff, clearly proves to us that a moderation of doctrine, dictated by charity, is not inconsistent with soundness in the faith. Such a sanction, I suppose, will be considered sufficient for the character of the remarks which I am about to make upon definitions in general, and upon the Vatican in particular.

The Vatican definition, which comes to us in the shape of the Pope's Encyclical Bull called the *Pastor Æternus*, declares that " the Pope has that same infallibility which the Church has :"* to determine therefore what is meant by the infallibility of the Pope we must turn first to consider the infallibility of the Church. And again, to determine the character of the Church's infallibility, we must consider what is the characteristic of Christianity, considered as a revelation of God's will.

Our Divine Master might have communicated to us heavenly truths without telling us that they came from Him, as it is commonly thought He has done in the case of heathen nations ; but He willed the Gospel to be a revelation acknowledged and authenticated, to be public, fixed, and permanent ; and accordingly, as Catholics hold, He framed a Society of men to be its home, its instrument, and its guarantee. The rulers of that Association are the legal trustees, so to say, of the sacred truths which He spoke to the Apostles by word of mouth. As He was leaving them, He gave them their great commission, and bade them "teach" their converts all over the earth, " to observe all things whatever He had commanded them;" and then He added, " Lo, I am with you always, even to the end of the world."

---

* Romanum Pontificem eâ infallibilitate pollere, quâ divinus Redemptor Ecclesiam suam in definiendâ doctrinâ de fide vel moribus instructam esse voluit.

Here, first, He told them to "teach" His revealed Truth; next, "to the consummation of all things;" thirdly, for their encouragement, He said that He would be with them "all days," all along, on every emergency or occasion, until that consummation. They had a duty put upon them of teaching their Master's words, a duty which they could not fulfil in the perfection which fidelity required, without His help; therefore came His promise to be with them in their performance of it. Nor did that promise of supernatural help end with the Apostles personally, for He adds, "to the consummation of the world," implying that the Apostles would have successors, and engaging that He would be with those successors as He had been with them.

The same safeguard of the Revelation—viz., an authoritative, permanent tradition of teaching is insisted on by an informant of equal authority with St. Matthew, but altogether independent of him, I mean St. Paul. He calls the Church "the pillar and ground of the Truth;" and he bids his convert Timothy, when he had become a ruler in that Church, to "take heed unto his doctrine," to "keep the deposit" of the faith, and to "commit" the things which he had heard from himself "to faithful men who should be fit to teach others."

This is how Catholics understand the Scripture record, nor does it appear how it can otherwise be understood; but, when we have got as far as this, and look back, we find that we have by implication made profession of a further doctrine. For, if the Church, initiated by the Apostles and continued in their successors, has been set up for the direct object of protecting, preserving, and declaring the Revelation, and that by means of the Guardianship and Providence of its Divine Author, we are led on to perceive that, in asserting this, we are in other words asserting, that, so far as the revealed message is concerned, the Church is infallible; for what is meant by infallibility in teaching but that the teacher in his teaching is secured from error? and how can fallible man be thus secured except by a supernatural infallible guidance? And what can have

H

been the object of the words, " I am with you all along to the end," but to give thereby an answer by anticipation to the spontaneous, silent alarm of the feeble company of fishermen and labourers, to whom they were addressed, on their finding themselves laden with superhuman duties and responsibilities.

Such then being, in its simple outline, the infallibility of the Church, such too will be the Pope's infallibility, as the Vatican Fathers have defined it. And if we find that by means of this outline we are able to fill out in all important respects the idea of a Council's infallibility, we shall thereby be ascertaining in detail what has been defined in 1870 about the infallibility of the Pope. With an attempt to do this I shall conclude.

1. The Church has the office of teaching, and the matter of that teaching is the body of doctrine, which the Apostles left behind them as her perpetual possession. If a question arises as to what the Apostolic doctrine is on a particular point, she has infallibility promised to her to enable her to answer correctly. And, as by the teaching of the Church is understood, not the teaching of this or that Bishop, but their united voice, and a Council is the form the Church must take, in order that all men may recognize that in fact she is teaching on any point in dispute, so in like manner the Pope must come before us in some special form or posture, if he is to be understood to be exercising his teaching office, and that form is called *ex cathedrâ*. This term is most appropriate, as being on one occasion used by our Lord Himself. When 'the Jewish doctors taught, they placed themselves in Moses' seat, and spoke *ex cathedrâ* ; and then, as He tells us, they were to be obeyed by their people, and that, whatever were their private lives or characters. " The Scribes and Pharisees," He says, " are seated on the chair of Moses : all things therefore whatsoever they shall say to you, observe and do ; but according to their works do you not, for they say and do not."

2. The forms, by which a General Council is identified

as representing the Church herself, are too clear to need drawing out; but what is to be that moral *cathedra*, or teaching chair, in which the Pope sits, when he is to be recognized as in the exercise of his infallible teaching? The new definition answers this question. He speaks *ex cathedrâ*, or infallibly, when he speaks, first, as the Universal Teacher; secondly, in the name and with the authority of the Apostles; thirdly, on a point of faith or morals; fourthly, with the purpose of binding every member of the Church to accept and believe his decision.

3. These conditions of course contract the range of his infallibility most materially. Hence Billuart speaking of the Pope, says, " Neither in conversation, nor in discussion, nor in interpreting Scripture or the Fathers, nor in consulting, nor in giving his reasons for the point which he has defined, nor in answering letters, nor in private deliberations, supposing he is setting forth his own opinion, is the Pope infallible," t. ii., p. 110.* And for this simple reason, because, on these various occasions of speaking his mind, he is not in the chair of the universal doctor.

4. Nor is this all; the greater part of Billuart's negatives refer to the Pope's utterances when he is out of the *Cathedra Petri*, but even, when he is in it, his words do not necessarily proceed from his infallibility. He has no wider prerogative than a Council, and of a Council Perrone says, "Councils are not infallible in the reasons by which they are led, or on which they rely, in making their definition, nor in matters which relate to persons, nor to physical matters which have no necessary connexion with dogma." *Prœl. Theol.* t. 2, p. 492. Thus, if a Council has condemned a work of Origen or Theodoret, it did not in so condemning go beyond the work itself; it did not touch the persons of either. Since this holds of a Council, it also holds in the case of the Pope; therefore, supposing a Pope has quoted the so-called works of the Areopagite as if really

* And so Fessler: " The Pope is not infallible as a man, or a theologian, or a priest, or a bishop, or a temporal prince, or a judge, or a legislator, or in his political views, or even in his government of the Church."—*Introd.*

genuine, there is no call on us to believe him; nor again, when he condemned Galileo's Copernicanism, unless the earth's immobility has a "necessary connexion with some dogmatic truth," which the present bearing of the Holy See towards that philosophy virtually denies.

5. Nor is a Council infallible, even in the prefaces and introductions to its definitions. There are theologians of name, as Tournely and Amort,* who contend that even those most instructive *capitula* passed in the Tridentine Council, from which the Canons with anathemas are drawn up, are not portions of the Church's infallible teaching; and the parallel introductions prefixed to the Vatican anathemas have an authority not greater nor less than that of those capitula.

6. Such passages, however, as these are too closely connected with the definitions themselves, not to be what is sometimes called, by a *catachresis*, "proximum fidei;" still, on the other hand, it is true also that, in those circumstances and surroundings of formal definitions, which I have been speaking of, whether of a Council or a Pope, there may be not only no exercise of an infallible voice, but actual error. Thus, in the Third Council, a passage of an heretical author was quoted in defence of the doctrine defined, under the belief he was Pope Julius, and narratives, not trustworthy, are introduced into the Seventh.

This remark and several before it will become intelligible if we consider that neither Pope nor Council are on a level with the Apostles. To the Apostles the whole revelation was given, by the Church it is transmitted; no simply new truth has been given to us since St. John's death; the one office of the Church is to guard "that noble deposit" of truth, as St. Paul speaks to Timothy, which the. Apostles bequeathed to her, in its fulness and integrity. Hence the infallibility of the Apostles was of a far more positive and wide character than that needed by and granted to the Church. We call it, in the case of the Apostles, inspiration; in the case of the Church *assistentia*.

* *Vid.* Amort. Dem. Cr., pp. 205—6.   This applies to the Unam Sanctam, *vid.* Fessler.

Of course there is a sense of the word "inspiration" in which it is common to all members of the Church, and therefore especially to its Bishops, and still more directly to its rulers, when solemnly called together in Council after much prayer throughout Christendom, and in a frame of mind especially serious and earnest by reason of the work they have in hand. The Paraclete certainly is ever with them, and more effectively in a Council, as being "in Spiritu Sancto congregata;" but I speak of the special and promised aid necessary for their fidelity to Apostolic teaching; and, in order to secure this fidelity, no inward gift of infallibility is needed, such as the Apostles had, no direct suggestion of divine truth, but simply an external guardianship, keeping them off from error (as a man's Guardian Angel, without enabling him to walk, might, on a night journey, keep him from pitfalls in his way), a guardianship saving them, as far as their ultimate decisions are concerned, from the effects of their inherent infirmities, from any chance of extravagance, of confusion of thought, of collision with former decisions or with Scripture, which in seasons of excitement might reasonably be feared.

"Never," says Perrone, "have Catholics taught that the gift of infallibility is given by God to the Church after the manner of inspiration."—t. 2, p. 253. Again: "[Human] media of arriving at the truth are excluded neither by a Council's nor by a Pope's infallibility, for God has promised it, not by way of an infused" or habitual "gift, but by the way of *assistentia*."—*ibid.* p. 541.

But since the process of defining truth is human, it is open to the chance of error; what Providence has guaranteed is only this, that there should be no error in the final step, in the resulting definition or dogma.

7. Accordingly, all that a Council, and all that the Pope, is infallible in, is the direct answer to the special question which he happens to be considering; his prerogative does not extend beyond a power, when in his *Cathedra*, of giving that very answer truly. "Nothing," says Perrone, "but the *objects* of dogmatic definitions of Councils are immutable, for in these are Councils infallible, not in their *reasons*," &c.—*ibid.*

8. This rule is so strictly to be observed that, though dogmatic statements are found from time to time in a Pope's Apostolic Letters, &c., yet they are not accounted to be exercises of his infallibility if they are said only *obiter*—by the way, and without direct intention to define. A striking instance of this *sine qua non* condition is afforded by Nicholas I., who, in a letter to the Bulgarians, spoke as if baptism were valid, when administered simply in our Lord's Name, without distinct mention of the Three Persons; but he is not teaching and speaking *ex cathedrâ*, because no question on this matter was in any sense the occasion of his writing. The question asked of him was concerning the *minister* of baptism—viz., whether a Jew or Pagan could validly baptize; in answering in the affirmative, he added *obiter*, as a private doctor, says Bellarmine, "that the baptism was valid, whether administered in the name of the three Persons or in the name of Christ only." (*de Rom. Pont.*, iv. 12.)

9. Another limitation is given in Pope Pius's own conditions set down in the *Pastor Æternus*, for the exercise of infallibility: viz., the proposition defined will be without any claim to be considered binding on the belief of Catholics, unless it is referable to the Apostolic *depositum*, through the channel either of Scripture or Tradition; and, though the Pope is the judge whether it is so referable or not, yet the necessity of his professing to abide by this reference is in itself a certain limitation of his dogmatic action. A Protestant will object indeed that, after his distinctly asserting that the Immaculate Conception and the Papal Infallibility are in Scripture and Tradition, this safeguard against erroneous definitions is not worth much, nor do I say that it is one of the most effective; but any how, in consequence of it, no Pope any more than a Council, could, for instance, introduce Ignatius's Epistles into the Canon of Scripture;—and, as to his dogmatic condemnation of particular books, which, of course, are foreign to the *depositum*, I would say, that, as to their false doctrine there can be no difficulty in condemning that, by means of that Apostolic deposit; nor surely in his condemning the very wording, in which they convey it, when

the subject is carefully considered. For the Pope's condemning the language, for instance, of Jansenius is a parallel act to the Church's receiving the word " Consubstantial," and if a Council and the Pope were not infallible so far in their judgment of language, neither Pope nor Council could draw up a dogmatic definition at all, for the right exercise of words is involved in the right exercise of thought.

10. And in like manner, as regards the precepts concerning moral duties, it is not in every such precept that the Pope is infallible. As a definition of faith must be drawn from the Apostolic *depositum* of doctrine, in order that it may be considered an exercise of infallibility, whether in the Pope or a Council, so too a precept of morals, if it is to be accepted as dogmatic, must be drawn from the Moral law, that primary revelation to us from God.

That is, in the first place, it must relate to things in themselves good or evil. If the Pope prescribed lying or revenge, his command would simply go for nothing, as if he had not issued it, because he has no power over the Moral Law. If he forbade his flock to eat any but vegetable food, or to dress in a particular fashion (questions of decency and modesty not coming into the question), he would in like manner be going beyond his province, because such a rule does not relate to a matter in itself good or bad. If he gave a precept all over the world for the adoption of lotteries instead of tithes or offerings, certainly it would be very hard to prove that he was contradicting the Moral Law, or ruling a practice to be in itself good which was in itself evil. There are few persons but would allow that it is at least doubtful whether lotteries are abstractedly evil, and in a doubtful matter the Pope is to be believed and obeyed.

However, there are other conditions besides this, necessary for the exercise of Papal infallibility in moral subjects:—for instance, his definition must relate to things necessary for salvation. No one would so speak of lotteries, nor of a particular dress, or of a particular kind of food;—such precepts, then, did he make them, would be simply external to the range of his prerogative.

And again, his infallibility in consequence is not called into exercise, unless he speaks to the whole world ; for, if his precepts, in order to be dogmatic, must enjoin what is necessary to salvation, they must be necessary for all men. Accordingly orders which issue from him for the observance of particular countries, or political or religious classes, have no claim to be the utterances of his infallibility. If he enjoins upon the hierarchy of Ireland to withstand mixed education, this is no exercise of his infallibility.

It may be added that the field of morals contains so little that is unknown and unexplored, in contrast with revelation and doctrinal fact, which form the domain of faith, that it is difficult to say what portions of moral teaching in the course of 1800 years actually have proceeded from the Pope, or from the Church, or where to look for such.   Nearly all that either oracle has done in this respect, has been to condemn such propositions as in a moral point of view are false, or dangerous, or rash ; and these condemnations, besides being such as in fact, will be found to command the assent of most men, as soon as heard, do not necessarily go so far as to present any positive statements for universal acceptance.

11. With the mention of condemned propositions I am brought to another and large consideration, which is one of the best illustrations that I can give of that principle of minimizing so necessary, as I think, for a wise and cautious theology ; at the same time I cannot insist upon it in the connexion into which I am going to introduce it, without submitting myself to the correction of divines more learned than I can pretend to be myself.

The infallibility, whether of the Church or of the Pope, acts principally or solely in two channels, in direct statements of truth, and in the condemnation of error.   The former takes the shape of doctrinal definitions, the latter stigmatizes propositions as heretical, next to heresy, erroneous, and the like.   In each case the Church, as guided by her Divine Master, has made provision for weighing as lightly as possible on the faith and conscience of her children.

As to the condemnation of propositions all she tells us is, that the thesis condemned when taken as a whole, or, again, when viewed in its context, is heretical, or blasphemous, or impious, or whatever other epithet she affixes to it. We have only to trust her so far as to allow ourselves to be warned against the thesis, or the work containing it. Theologians employ themselves in determining what precisely it is that is condemned in that thesis or treatise ; and doubtless in most cases they do so with success ; but that determination is not *de fide* ; all that is of faith is that there is in that thesis itself, which is noted, heresy or error, or other peccant matter, as the case may be, such, that the censure is a peremptory command to theologians, preachers, students, and all other whom it concerns, to keep clear of it. But so light is this obligation, that instances frequently occur, when it is successfully maintained by some new writer, that the Pope's act does not imply what it has seemed to imply, and questions which seemed to be closed, are after a course of years re-opened. In discussions such as these, there is a real exercise of private judgment, and an allowable one ; the act of faith, which cannot be superseded or trifled with, being, I repeat, the unreserved acceptance that the thesis in question is heretical, or erroneous in faith, &c., as the Pope or the Church has spoken of it.

In these cases which in a true sense may be called the Pope's *negative* enunciations, the opportunity of a legitimate minimizing lies in the intensely concrete character of the matters condemned ; in his affirmative enunciations a like opportunity is afforded by their being more or less abstract. Indeed, excepting such as relate to persons, that is, to the Trinity in Unity, the Blessed Virgin, the Saints, and the like, all the dogmas of Pope or of Council are but general, and so far, in consequence, admit of exceptions in their actual application,—these exceptions being determined either by other authoritative utterances, or by the scrutinizing vigilance, acuteness, and subtlety of the *Schola Theologorum.*

One of the most remarkable instances of what I am

insisting on is found in a dogma, which no Catholic can
ever think of disputing, viz., that " Out of the Church,
and out of the faith, is no salvation." Not to go to
Scripture, it is the doctrine of St. Ignatius, St. Irenæus,
St. Cyprian in the first three centuries, as of St. Augustine and his contemporaries in the fourth and fifth. It
can never be other than an elementary truth of Christianity; and the present Pope has proclaimed it as all
Popes, doctors, and bishops before him. But that truth
has two aspects, according as the force of the negative
falls upon the " Church " or upon the " salvation." The
main sense is, that there is no other communion or so-
called Church, but the Catholic, in which are stored the
promises, the sacraments and other means of salvation ;
the other and derived sense is, that no one can be saved
who is not in that one and only Church. But it does
not follow, because there is no Church but one which
has the Evangelical gifts and privileges to bestow, that
therefore no one can be saved without the intervention
of that one Church. Anglicans quite understand this
distinction ; for, on the one hand, their Article says,
" They are to be had accursed (anathematizandi) that
presume to say, that every man shall be saved *by* (in)
the law or sect which he professeth, so that he be dili-
gent to frame his life according to that law and the light
of nature ;" while on the other hand they speak of and
hold the doctrine of the "uncovenanted mercies of God."
The latter doctrine in its Catholic form is the doctrine of
invincible ignorance—or, that it is possible to belong to
the soul of the Church without belonging to the body ;
and, at the end of 1,800 years, it has been formally
and authoritatively put forward by the present Pope
(the first Pope, I suppose, who has done so,) on the
very same occasion on which he has repeated the funda-
mental principle of exclusive salvation itself. It is to the
purpose here to quote his words ; they occur in the course
of his Encyclical, addressed to the Bishops of Italy, under
date of August 10, 1863.

  " *We and you know*, that those who lie under invincible ignorance as regards our most Holy Religion, and who, diligently observing the natural law, and its precepts, which are engraven by God on the hearts of all, and prepared to obey God, lead a good and upright life, are able, by the operation of the power of divine light and grace, to obtain eternal life."*

Who would at first sight gather from the wording of so forcible a universal, that an exception to its operation, such as this, so distinct, and, for what we know, so very wide, was consistent with holding it?

Another instance of a similar kind is the general acceptance in the Latin Church, since the time of St. Augustine, of the doctrine of absolute predestination, as instanced in the teaching of other great saints besides him, such as St. Fulgentius, St. Prosper, St. Gregory, St. Thomas, and St. Buonaventure. Yet in the last centuries a great explanation and modification of this doctrine has been effected by the efforts of the Jesuit School, which have issued in the reception of a distinction between predestination to grace and predestination to glory; and a consequent admission of the principle that, though our own works do not avail for bringing us into a state of salvation on earth, they do avail, when in that state of salvation or grace, for our attainment of eternal glory in heaven. Two saints of late centuries, St. Francis de Sales and St. Alfonso, seem to have professed this less rigid opinion, which is now the more common doctrine of the day.

Another instance is supplied by the Papal decisions concerning Usury. Pope Clement V., in the Council of Vienne, declares, "If any one shall have fallen into the error of pertinaciously presuming to affirm•that usury is no sin, we determine that he is to be punished as a heretic." However, in the year 1831 the Sacred *Pœnitentiaria* answered an inquiry on the subject, to the effect that

---

* The Pope speaks more forcibly still in an earlier Allocution. After mentioning invincible ignorance he adds :—" Quis tantum sibi arroget, ut hujusmodi ignorantiæ designare limites queat, juxta populorum, regionum, ingeniorum, aliarumque rerum tam multarum rationem et varietatem ?"—*Dec.* 9, 1854.

the Holy See suspended its decision on the point, and that a confessor who allowed of usury was not to be disturbed, "non esse inquietandum." Here again a double aspect seems to have been realized of the idea intended by the word *usury*.

To show how natural this process of partial and gradually developed teaching is, we may refer to the apparent contradiction of Bellarmine, who says "the Pope, whether he can err or not, is to be obeyed by all the faithful," (*Rom. Pont.* iv. 2), yet, as I have quoted him above, p. 52-53, sets down (ii. 29) cases in which he is not to be obeyed. An illustration may be given in political history in the discussions which took place years ago as to the force of the Sovereign's Coronation Oath to uphold the Established Church. The words were large and general, and seemed to preclude any act on his part to the prejudice of the Establishment; but lawyers succeeded at length in making a distinction between the legislative and executive action of the Crown, which is now generally accepted.

These instances out of many similar are sufficient to show what caution is to be observed, on the part of private and unauthorized persons, in imposing upon the consciences of others any interpretation of dogmatic enunciations which is beyond the legitimate sense of the words, inconsistent with the principle that all general rules have exceptions, and unrecognized by the Theological *Schola*.

12. From these various considerations it follows, that Papal and Synodal definitions, obligatory on our faith, are of rare occurrence ; and this is confessed by all sober theologians. Father O'Reilly, for instance, of Dublin, one of the first theologians of the day, says :—

"The Papal Infallibility is comparatively seldom brought into action. I am very far from denying that the Vicar of Christ is largely assisted by God in the fulfilment of his sublime office, that he receives great light and strength to do well the great work entrusted to him and imposed on him, that he is continually guided from above in the government of the Catholic Church. But this is not the meaning of Infallibility... What is the use of dragging in the Infallibility in connexion with Papal acts with which it has nothing to do ? Papal acts, which are very good and very holy, and entitled to all respect and obedience, acts in which the Pontiff is commonly not mistaken, but in which he could be mistaken and still remain infallible in the only sense in which he has been declared to be so." (The *Irish Monthly*, Vol. ii. No. 10, 1874.)*

This great authority goes on to disclaim any desire to minimize, but there is, I hope, no real difference between us here. He, I am sure, would sanction me in my repugnance to impose upon the faith of others more than what the Church distinctly claims of them : and I should follow him in thinking it a more scriptural, Christian, dutiful, happy frame of mind, to be easy, than to be difficult, of belief. I have already spoken of that uncatholic spirit, which starts with a grudging faith in the word of the Church, and determines to hold nothing but what it is, as if by demonstration, compelled to believe. To be a true Catholic a man must have a generous loyalty towards ecclesiastical authority, and accept what is taught him with what is called the *pietas fidei,* and only such a tone of mind has a claim, and it certainly has a claim, to be met and to be handled with a wise and gentle *minimism.* Still the fact remains, that there has been of late years a fierce and intolerant temper abroad, which scorns and virtually tramples on the little ones of Christ.

I end with an extract from the Pastoral of the Swiss Bishops, a Pastoral which has received the Pope's approbation.

"It in no way depends upon the caprice of the Pope, or upon his good pleasure, to make such and such a doctrine, the object of a dogmatic definition. He is tied up and limited to the divine revelation, and to the truths which that revelation contains. He is tied up and limited by the

* *Vid.* Fessler also ; and I believe Father Perrone says the same.

Creeds, already in existence, and by the preceding definitions of the Church. He is tied up and limited by the
divine law, and by the constitution of the Church. Lastly,
he is tied up and limited by that doctrine, divinely revealed,
which affirms that alongside religious society there is civil
society, that alongside the Ecclesiastical Hierarchy, there is
the power of temporal Magistrates, invested in their own
domain with a full sovereignty, and to whom we owe
obedience in conscience, and respect in all things morally
permitted, and belonging to the domain of civil society."

§ 10. Conclusion.

I have now said all that I consider necessary in order to fulfil the task which I have undertaken, a task very painful to me and ungracious. I account it a great misfortune, that my last words, as they are likely to be, should be devoted to a controversy with one whom I have always so much respected and admired. But I should not have been satisfied with myself, if I had not responded to the call made upon me from such various quarters, to the opportunity at last given me of breaking a long silence on subject deeply interesting to me, and to the demands of my own honour.

The main point of Mr. Gladstone's charge against us is that in 1870, after a series of preparatory acts, a great change and irreversible was effected in the political attitude of the Church by the third and fourth chapters of the Vatican *Pastor Æternus*, a change which no state or statesman can afford to pass over. Of this cardinal assertion I consider he has given no proof at all ; and my object throughout the foregoing pages has been to make this clear. The Pope's infallibility indeed and his supreme authority have in the Vatican *capita* been declared matters of faith ; but his prerogative of infallibility lies in matters speculative, and his prerogative of authority is no infallibility, in laws, commands, or measures. His infallibility bears upon the domain of thought, not directly of action, and while it may fairly exercise the theologian, philosopher, or man of science, it scarcely concerns the politician. Moreover, whether the recognition of his infallibility in doctrine will increase his actual power over the faith of Catholics, remains to be seen, and must be determined by the event ; for there are gifts too large and too fearful to be handled freely. Mr. Gladstone seems to feel this, and therefore insists upon the increase made by the Vatican definition in the Pope's authority. But there is no real increase; he has for centuries upon centuries had and used that authority, which the Definition now declares ever to have belonged to him. Before the Council there was the rule of obedience, and there were exceptions to the rule; and since the Council the rule remains, and with it the possibility of exceptions.

It may be objected that a representation such as this, is negatived by the universal sentiment, which testifies to the formidable effectiveness of the Vatican decrees, and to the Pope's intention that they should be effective; that it is the boast of some Catholics and the reproach levelled against us by all Protestants, that the Catholic Church has now become beyond mistake a despotic aggressive Papacy, in which freedom of thought and action is utterly extinguished. But I do not allow this alleged unanimous testimony to exist. Of course Prince Bismarck and other statesmen such as Mr. Gladstone, rest their opposition to Pope Pius on the political ground; but the Old-Catholic movement is based, not upon politics, but upon theology, and Dr. Dollinger has more than once, I believe, declared his disapprobation of the Prussian acts against the Pope, while Father Hyacinth has quarrelled with the anti-Catholic politics of Geneva. The French indeed have shown their sense of the political support which the Holy Father's name and influence would bring to their country; but does any one suppose that they expect to derive support definitely from the Vatican decrees, and not rather from the *prestige* of that venerable Authority, which those decrees have rather lowered than otherwise in the eyes of the world? So again the Legitimists and Carlists in France and Spain doubtless wish to associate themselves with Rome; but where and how have they signified that they can turn to profit the special dogma of the Pope's infallibility, and would not have been better pleased to be rid of the controversy which it has occasioned? In fact, instead of there being a universal impression that the proclamation of his infallibility and supreme authority has strengthened the Pope's secular position in Europe, there is room for suspecting that some of the politicians of the day, (I do not mean Mr. Gladstone) were not sorry that the Ultramontane party was successful at the Council in their prosecution of an object which those politicians considered to be favourable to the interests of the Civil Power. There is certainly some plausibility in the view, that it is not the " Curia Romana," as Mr. Gladstone considers, or the ' Jesuits," who are the " astute " party, but that rather they are themselves victims of the astuteness of secular statesmen.

The recognition, which I am here implying, of the existence of parties in the Church reminds me of what, while I have been writing these pages, I have all along felt would be at once the *primâ facie* and also the most telling criticism upon me. It will be said that there are very considerable differences in argument and opinion between me and others who have replied to Mr. Gladstone, and I shall be taunted with the evident break-down, thereby made manifest, of that topic of glorification so commonly in the mouths of Catholics, that they are all of one way of thinking, while Protestants are all at variance with each other, and by that very variation of opinion can have no ground of certainty severally in their own.

This is a showy and serviceable retort in controversy; but it is nothing more. First, as regards the arguments which Catholics use, it has to be considered whether they are really incompatible with each other; if they are not, then surely it is generally granted by Protestants as well as Catholics, that two distinct arguments for the same conclusion, instead of invalidating that conclusion, actually strengthen it. And next, supposing the difference to be one of conclusions themselves, then it must be considered whether the difference relates to a matter of faith or to a matter of opinion. If a matter of faith is in question I grant there ought to be absolute agreement, or rather I maintain that there is; I mean to say that only one out of the statements put forth can be true, and that the other statements will be at once withdrawn by their authors, by virtue of their being Catholics, as soon as they

I

learn on good authority that they are erroneous. But if the differences which I have supposed are only in theological opinion, they do but show that after all private judgment is not so utterly unknown among Catholics and in Catholic Schools, as Protestants are desirous to establish.

I have written on this subject at some length in Lectures which I published many years ago, but, it would appear, with little practical effect upon those for whom they were intended. "Left to himself," I say, "each Catholic likes and would maintain his own opinion and his private judgment just as much as a Protestant; and he has it and he maintains it, just so far as the Church does not, by the authority of Revelation, supersede it. The very moment the Church ceases to speak, at the very point at which she, that is, God who speaks by her, circumscribes her range of teaching, then private judgment of necessity starts up; there is nothing to hinder it. . . . A Catholic sacrifices his opinion to the Word of God, declared through His Church; but from the nature of the case, there is nothing to hinder him having his own opinion and expressing it, whenever, and so far as, the Church, the oracle of Revelation, does not speak.*

In saying this, it must not be supposed that I am denying what is called the *pietas fidei*, that is, a sense of the great probability of the truth of enunciations made by the Church, which are not formally and actually to be considered as the "Word of God." Doubtless it is our duty to check many a speculation, or at least many an utterance, even though we are not bound to condemn it as contrary to religious truth. But, after all, the field of religious thought which the duty of faith occupies, is small indeed compared with that which is open to our free, though of course to our reverent and conscientious, speculation.

I draw from these remarks two conclusions; first as regards Protestants,—Mr. Gladstone should not on the one hand declaim against us as having "no mental freedom," if the periodical press on the other hand is to mock us as admitting a liberty of private judgment, purely Protestant. We surely are not open to contradictory imputations. Every note of triumph over the differences which mark our answers to Mr. Gladstone is a distinct admission that we do not deserve his injurious reproach that we are captives and slaves of the Pope.

Secondly, for the benefit of some Catholics, I would observe that, while I acknowledge one Pope, *jure divino*, I acknowledge no other, and that I think it a usurpation, too wicked to be comfortably dwelt upon, when individuals use their own private judgment, in the discussion of religious questions, not simply " abundare in suo sensu," but for the purpose of anathematizing the private judgment of others.

I say there is only one Oracle of God, the Holy Catholic Church and the Pope as her head. To her teaching I have ever desired all my thoughts, all my words to be conformed; to her judgment I submit what I have now written, what I have ever written, not only as regards its truth, but as to its prudence, its suitableness, and its expedience. I think I have not pursued any end of my own in anything that I have published, but I know well, that, in matters not of faith, I may have spoken, when I ought to have been silent.

And now, my dear Duke, I release you from this long discussion, and, in concluding, beg you to accept the best Christmas wishes and prayers for your present and future from

Your affectionate Friend and Servant,

JOHN HENRY NEWMAN.

The Oratory,
Dec. 27, 1874.

POSTSCRIPT.

February 26, 1875. Mr. Gladstone's new Pamphlet, which has just appeared, is only partially directed against the foregoing Letter, and, when he remarks on what I have written, he does so with a gentleness which may be thought to be unfair to his argument. Moreover, he commences with some pages about me personally of so special a character, that, did I dare dwell upon them in their direct import, they would of course gratify me exceedingly. But I cannot do so, because I believe that, with that seriousness which is characteristic of him, he has wished to say what he felt to be true, not what was complimentary ; and because, looking on beyond his words to what they imply, I see in them, though he did not mean it so himself, a grave, or almost a severe question addressed to me, which effectually keeps me from taking pleasure in them, however great is the honour they do me.

It is indeed a stern question which his words suggest, whether, now that I have come to the end of my days, I have used aright whatever talents God has given me, and as He would have had me use them, in building up religious truth, and not in pulling down, breaking up, and scattering abroad. All I can say in answer to it, is, that from the day I became a Catholic to this day, now close upon thirty years, I have never had a moment's misgiving that the communion of Rome is that Church which the Apostles set up at Pentecost, which alone has " the adoption of sons, and the glory, and the covenants,

K

and the revealed law, and the service of God, and the promises," and in which the Anglican communion, whatever
its merits and demerits, whatever the great excellence of
individuals in it, has, as such, no part. Nor have I ever for a
moment hesitated in my conviction since 1845, that it was my
clear duty to join that Catholic Church, as I did then join it,
which in my own conscience I felt to be divine. Persons and
places, incidents and circumstances of life, which belong to
my first fortyfour years, are deeply lodged in my memory and
my affections ; moreover, I have had more to try and afflict
me in various ways as a Catholic than as an Anglican ; but
never for a moment have I wished myself back; never have
I ceased to thank my Maker for His mercy in enabling me
to make the great change, and never has He let me feel for-
saken by Him, or in distress, or any kind of religious trouble.
I do not know how to avoid thus meeting Mr. Gladstone's
language about me : but I can say no more. The judgment must be left to a day to come.

In the remarks that follow I shall take the order of
my Sections.

§ 1.

My first reason for writing in answer to Mr. Gladstone's
Expostulation was his charge against us, "that Catholics,
if they act consistently with their principles, cannot be
loyal subjects," *supr.* p. 7. And he withdraws this in his new
Pamphlet, (*Vaticanism*, p. 14.) though not in very gracious
language, "The immediate purpose of my appeal," he
says, "has been attained, in so far that the loyalty of our
Roman Catholic fellow-subjects in the mass remains evidently untainted and secure."

My second reason was to protest against "his attack
upon our moral uprightness," *supr. ibid.* Here again he
seems to grant that, if what I say can be received as genuine

Catholic teaching, I have succeeded in my purpose. He has a doubt, however, whether it does not "smack of Protestantism," *Vat.* p. 69. He does not give any distinct reason for this doubt; and, though I shall notice it in its place, *infr.* § 5, I think it fair to maintain as a plain principle of controversy, that it is the accuser who has to prove his point, and that he must not content himself with professing that the accused parties have not succeeded to his satisfaction in disproving it.

Lastly, as springing out of these two charges and illustrating them, was his exaggerated notion of the force, drift, and range of the Vatican definition of the Pope's infallibility. Here again I consider he leaves my interpretation of it without reply, though apparently it does not content him. Some of the objections, which he throws out *obiter* to what I have said, shall now be noticed.

Supr. pp. 14, 15. I have said, apropos of the prospect of a definition of the Pope's Infallibility in the time of Pitt and Peel, "If [the government] wanted to obtain some real information about the probabilities of the future, why did they not go to head quarters? why not go to Rome? ...... It is impossible that they could have entered into formal negociations with the Pope, without its becoming perfectly clear that Rome could never be a party to such a a pledge as England wanted, and that no pledge from Catholics was of value to which Rome was not a party." To my astonishment Mr. Gladstone seems to consider this a fatal admission. He cries out, "Statesmen of the future recollect the words! . . The lesson received is this : although pledges were given, although their validity was formally and even passionately asserted, although the subject matter was one of civil allegiance, 'no pledge from Catholics was of any value, to which Rome was not a party.'" p. 39.

I deny that the question of infallibility was one
of civil allegiance, but let that pass; as to the main
principle involved in what I have said, it certainly
does perplex and confuse me that a statesman with Mr.
Gladstone's experience should make light of credentials, and
should not recognize the difference between party opinion
and formal decisions and pledges. What is the use of ac-
credited ministers and an official intercourse between foreign
powers, if the acts of mere classes or interests will do instead
of them? At a congress, I believe the first act of pleni-
potentiaries is to show to each other their credentials.
What minister of foreign affairs would go to the Cesaro-
witch, who happened to be staying among us, for an explanation of an expedition of Russia in upper Asia, instead
of having recourse to the Russian ambassador?

The common saying, that "Whigs are Tories out
of place" illustrates again what is in itself so axio-
matic. Successive ministries of opposite views show
in history, for the most part, as one consistent national government, and, when a foreign power mistakes
the objections which public men in opposition make
to the details, circumstances, or seasonableness of certain
ministerial measures, for deliberate judgments in its
favour, it is likely, as in the case of the great Napoleon, to incur eventually, when the opposition comes
into office, great disappointment, and has no one to
blame but itself. So again, the Czar Nicholas seems to
have mistaken the deputation of the peace party before the
Crimean war for the voice of the English nation. It is not
a business-like way of acting to assume the assurances of
partizans, however sincerely made, for conditions of a contract. There is nothing indeed to show that the Holy See
in 1793 or 1829 had any notion that the infallibility of the
Pope, if ever made a dogma, would be so made within

such limits of time as could affect the *bonâ fide* character of
the prospects which English and Irish Catholics opened upon
Mr. Pitt or Mr. Peel. The events in Europe of the foregoing
half century gave no encouragement to the Papal cause.
Nor did Catholics alone avow anticipations which helped to
encourage the latter statesman in the course, into which
the political condition of Ireland, not any kindness to the
Irish religion, primarily turned him. There were Anglican
ecclesiastics, whom he deservedly trusted, who gave it to
him as their settled opinion, as regards the Protestantism of
England, that, if the emancipation of Catholics could but be
passed in the night, there would be no excitement about it
next morning. Did such an influential judgment, thus
offered to Mr. Peel, involve a breach of a pledge, because it
was not fulfilled ?

It was notorious all over the world that the North of
Catholic Christendom took a different view of Papal infallibility from the South. A long controversy had gone on;
able writers were to be found on either side; each side was
positive in the truth of its own cause; each hoped to prevail. The Gallican party, towards which England and
Ireland inclined, thought the other simply extravagant; but
with the Ultramontane stood Rome itself. Ministers do not
commonly believe all the representations of deputations
who come to them with the advocacy of particular measures, though those deputations may be perfectly sincere
in what they aver. The Catholics of England and Ireland in 1826 were almost as one man in thinking lightly
of the question, but even then there were those who
spoke out in a different sense, and warned the government that there was a contrary opinion, and one strong
both in its pretensions and in its prospects. I am not
bound to go into this subject at length, for I have allowed
the dominant feeling among our Catholics at that day was

against the prudence or likelihood of a definition of Papal
infallibility ; but I will instance one or two writers of name
who had spoken in a different sense.

I cannot find that Mr. Gladstone deals with my reference to Archbishop Troy, whose pastoral bears the date
(1793) of the very year in which, as Mr. Gladstone tells
us, *Vat.* p. 48, a Relief Act was granted to Ireland. The
Archbishop, as the passage has been found for me, says,
" *Many* Catholics contend that the Pope . . is infallible
. . others deny this. . . . *Until* the Church shall *decide*
. . . either opinion may be adopted." *Supr.*, pp. 12, 13.
This is a very significant, as well as authoritative passage.

Again :—Father Mumford's *Catholic Scripturist* is a
popular Address to Protestants, in the vernacular, which
has gone through various editions in the 17th, 18th, and
19th centuries. The edition from which I quote is that
of 1863. He says, p. 39, " Whether the definition of a
council alone, defining without their chief pastor, or the
definition of the chief pastor alone, defining without a
council, be infallible or no, there be several opinions
amongst us, in which we do and may vary without any
prejudice to our faith, which is not built upon what is *yet*
under opinion, but upon that which is delivered as infallible."

Again, Bishop Hay is one of the most conspicuous
Prelates and authoritative writers amongst us of the 18th
century. In his *"Sincere Christian,"* published between
1770 and 1780, he treats of the infallibility of the Pope at
considerable length, and in its favour. He says, p. 188
(*ed.* 1871) that that doctrine "is not proposed to us as an
article of divine faith, nor has the Church ever made
any decision concerning it. Great numbers of the most
learned divines are of opinion that in such a case, the
Head of the Church is infallible in what he teaches, but

there are others who are of a contrary opinion." He proceeds, "On what grounds do those divines found their opinion, who believe that the Pope himself, when he speaks to the faithful as head of the church, is infallible in what he teaches?" and he answers, "On very strong reasons both from Scripture, tradition, and reason." These he goes through *seriatim*; then he adds, p. 194, "What proof do the others bring for their opinion, that the Head of the Church is not infallible? They bring not a single text of Scripture, nor almost one argument from tradition to prove it."

I might add that the chief instrument in rousing and rallying the Protestant sentiment against Catholic emancipation was from first to last the episcopate and clergy of the Church Established; now, if there was any body of men who were perfectly aware of the division of sentiment among Catholics as to the seat of infallibility, it was they. Their standard divines, writing in the vernacular, discharge it, as one of their most effective taunts, against their opponents, that, whilst the latter hold the doctrine of infallibility, they differ among themselves whether it is lodged in an Ecumenical Council or in the Roman See. It never can be said then that this opinion, which has now become a dogma, was not perfectly well known to be living and energetic in the Catholic communion, though it was not an article of faith, and was not spoken of as such by Catholics in this part of the world during the centuries of persecution.

Mr. Gladstone, as his mildest conclusion against us, is inclined to grant that it was not an act of duplicity in us, that in 1826 our Prelates spoke against the Pope's infallibility, though in 1870 they took part in defining it; but then he maintains it to be at least a proof that the Church has changed its doctrine, and thereby forfeited its claim to be "semper eadem." But it is no change surely to decide between two prevalent opinions; but, if it is to be so regarded, then change has been the characteristic of the church from the earliest times, as, for instance, in the third century, on the point of the validity of baptism by heretics. And hence such change as has taken place, (which I should prefer to call doctrinal development,) is in itself a positive argument in favour of the Church's identity from first to last; for a growth in its creed is a law of its life. I have already insisted upon this, *supra*, p. 120; also in former volumes, as in my *Apologia*, and *Difficulties of Anglicans.*

§ 3.

Supr. p. 28. As Mr. Gladstone denied that the Papal prerogatives were consistent with ancient history, I said in answer that that history on the contrary was the clearest witness in their favour, as showing how the promises made to St. Peter were providentially fulfilled by political, &c., changes, external to the Pope, which worked for him. I did not mean to deny that those prerogatives were his from the beginning, but merely that they were gradually brought into full exercise by a course of events, which history records. Thus it was a mistake to say that Catholics could not appeal in favour of the Papal power to history. To make my meaning quite clear, as I hoped, I distinctly said I was not speaking theologically, but historically, nay, looking at the state of things with " non-Catholic eyes." However, as the following passage from the *Etudes Religieuses* shews, it seems that I have been misunderstood, though the writer himself, Père Ramière, does me the justice and the favour to defend me, and I here adopt his words as my defence. He says:

"Pour exprimer cette concentration providentielle, dans les mains du Pape, du pouvoir ecclésiastique partagé autrefois dans une plus large mesure par l'épiscopat, le P. Newman se sert d'un terme légal qu'il ne faut évidemment pas prendre à la lettre. Il dit que le Pape est *héritier par défaut* de la hiérarchie œcuménique du iv\ siècle. Le savant directeur de la *Voce della Verità* blâme cette expression, qui impliquerait, selon lui, que le Pape tient son pouvoir de la hiérarchie. Mais le P. Newman exclut cette interprétation, puis qu'il fait deriver la plénitude du pouvoir pontifical de la promesse faite par Jésus-Christ à Saint Pierre," p. 256, 7, note.

§ 4.

Supr. p. 58. I here say that "were I actually a soldier or sailor in her Majesty's service in a just war, and should the Pope suddenly bid all Catholic soldiers and sailors to retire from her service, taking the advice, &c., . . I should not obey him." Here I avail myself of a passage in Canon Neville's recent pamphlet (" A few Comments, &c., *Pickering*) in which he speaks with the authority belonging to a late theological Professor of Maynooth :

" In the impossible hypothesis of the Pope being engaged in a war with England, how would the allegiance of English Catholics be affected ? . . how would it be, if they were soldiers or sailors ? . . . . Some one will urge, the Pope may issue a mandate enforced by an annexed excommunication, forbidding all Catholics to engage in the war against him . . . The supposed action of the Pope does not change the question materially. His mandate will derive its force from his authoritative declaration of the immorality of the war, and the censures annexed," *i. e.* excommunication, "will have to be subjected to the ordinary rules and principles of ecclesiastical punishments. For instance, the soldiers and sailors would not incur it, because '*grave fears*' excuse from censure [excommunication], censures being directed against the contumacious, not against those who act through fear or coercion . . . It is a trite principle, that mere ecclesiastical laws do not bind, when there would be a very grave inconvenience in their observance ; and it denies as a rule to any human legislator (*e.g.*, the Pope) the power of making laws or precepts, binding men to the performance of actions, which, from the danger and difficulty attendant on their fulfilment, are esteemed heroic," pp. 101, 2.

§ 5.

Supr. p. 61. I have said, " The Pope who comes of Revelation, has no jurisdiction over Nature," *i.e.* the natural Law. Mr. Gladstone on the other hand says, " Idle it is to tell us, finally, that the Pope is bound by the moral and divine law, by the commandments of God, by the rules of the Gospel : . . . for of these, one and all, the Pope himself, by himself, is the judge without appeal." p. 102. That is, Mr. Gladstone thinks that the Pope may deny and anathematize the proposition, "There is one God :" and may proceed to circulate by Cardinal Antonelli a whole Syllabus of kindred " erroneous theses" for the instructions of the Bishops. Catholics think this impossible, as believing in a Divine Providence ever exercised over the Church. But let us grant, for argument-sake, that a Pope could commit so insane a violation of the Natural and the Revealed Law:—we know what would be the consequence to such a Pope. Cardinal Turrecremata teaches, as I have quoted him, that " were the Pope to command any thing against Holy Scripture, or the articles of faith, or the truth of the Sacraments, or the commands of the natural or divine law, he ought not to be obeyed, but in such commands to be ignored." *Supr.* p. 52. Other, and they the highest Ultramontane theologians, hold that a Pope, who teaches heresy, *ipso facto* ceases to be Pope.

Supr. p. 66. Here, after stating that there are cases in which the Pope's commands are to be resisted by individual Catholics, I challenge Mr. Gladstone to bring passages from our authoritative writers to the contrary: and I add, "they must be passages declaring not only that the Pope is ever to be obeyed, but that there are no exceptions to this rule, for exceptions ever must be in all concrete matters." Instead of doing so, Mr. Gladstone contents himself with enunciating the contradictory to what I have said. "Dr. Newman says there are exceptions to this precept of obedience. But this is just what the Council has not said. The Church by the Council imposes Aye. The private conscience reserves to itself the title to say No. I must confess that in this apology there is to me a strong, undeniable, smack of Protestantism." p. 69.

Mr. Gladstone says "there is to me ;" yes, certainly to him and other Protestants, because they do not know our doctrine. I have given in my Pamphlet, three reasons in justification of what I said ; first that exceptions *must* be from the nature of the case, "for in *all* concrete matters," not only in precepts of obedience, rules are but general, and exceptions must occur. Then, in a later page, p. 121, I give actual instances, which have occurred in the history of Catholic teaching, of exceptions after large principles have been laid down. But my main reason lies in the absolute statements of theologians. I willingly endure to have about me a smack of Protestantism, which attaches to Cardinal Turrecremata in the 15th century, to Cardinals Jacobatius and Bellarmine in the 16th, to the Carmelites of Salamanca in the 17th, and to all theologians prior to them ; and also to the whole Schola after them, such as to Fathers Corduba, Natalis Alexander and Busenbaum, and so down to St. Alfonso Liguori the latest Doctor of the Church in the 18th, and to Cardinal Gousset and to Archbishop Kenrick in the 19th.

§ 6.

Supr. pp. 76, 77. Speaking ·of the proposition condemned in the Encyclical ·of 1864, to the effect that it is
the right of any one to have liberty to give public utterance,
in every possible shape, by every possible channel, without
any let or hindrance from God or man, to all his notions
whatever, I have said that "it seems a light epithet for
the Pope to use, when he calls such a doctrine of conscience
a *deliramentum.*" Presently I add, "Perhaps Mr. Gladstone will say, Why should the Pope take the trouble to
condemn what is so wild ? but he does," &c.

On this Mr. Gladstone remarks *Vat.* p. 21, 22. "It
appears to me that this is, to use a mild phrase, merely
trifling with the subject. We are asked to believe that
what the Pope intended to condemn was a state of things
which never has existed in any country in the world. Now
he says he is condemning one of the commonly prevailing
errors of the time, familiarly known to the Bishops whom
he addresses. What bishop knows of a State which by law
allows a perfectly free course to blasphemy, filthiness, and
sedition ?"

I do not find any thing to show that the Pope is speaking of States, and not of writers ; and, though I do not
pretend to know against what writers he is speaking, yet
there are writers who do maintain doctrines which carried
out consistently would reach that *deliramentum* which the
Pope speaks of, if they have not rather already·reached it.
We are a sober people ; but are not the doctrines of even
so grave and patient a thinker as the late Mr. J. S. Mill
very much in that direction ? He says, "The appropriate
region of human liberty comprises first the inward domain
of consciousness; demanding liberty of conscience in the
most comprehensive sense, liberty of thought and feeling,

absolute freedom of opinion and sentiment on all subjects practical or speculative, scientific, moral, or theological. The liberty of *expressing* and *publishing* opinion may *seem* to fall under a different principle, since it belongs to that part of the conduct of an individual which concerns other people ; but, being almost of as much importance as the liberty of thought itself, and resting in great part on the same reasons, *is practically inseparable from it,* &c. &c. . . No society in which these liberties are not on the whole respected, is free, whatever may be its form of government," (*On Liberty, Introd.*) Of course he does not allow of a freedom to harm others, though we have to consider well what he means by harming : but it is a freedom which must meet with no "impediment from our fellow creatures, so long as what we do does not harm them, even though they should think our conduct foolish, perverse, or wrong." "The only freedom," he continues, "which deserves the name is that of pursuing our own good in our own way, so long as we do not attempt to deprive others of theirs, or impede their efforts to obtain it. Each is the proper guardian of his own health, whether bodily, or mental and spiritual."

That is, no immoral doctrines, poems, novels, plays, conduct, acts, may be visited by the reprobation of public opinion ; nothing must be put down, I do not say by the laws, but even by society, by the press, by religious influence, merely on the ground of shocking the sense of decency and the modesty of a Christian community. Nay, the police must not visit Holywell Street, nor a license be necessary for dancing rooms : but the most revolting atrocities of heathen times and countries must for conscience-sake be allowed free exercise in our great cities. Averted looks indeed and silent disgust, or again rational expostulation, is admissible against them, but nothing of a more energetic character.

I do not impute this to Mr. Mill. He had too much English common sense to carry out his principles to these extreme but legitimate conclusions ;. he strove to find means of limiting them by the introduction of other and antagonist principles ; but then that such a man held the theory of liberty which he has avowed, and that he has a great following, is a suggestion to us that the Holy See may have had abundant reason in the present state of the continent to anathematize a proposition which to Mr. Gladstone seems so wild and unheard of.

Supra, pp. 79, 82. I have said that the Syllabus is to be received from the Pope with " profound submission," p. 79, and " by an act of obedience," p. 82; I add, "but not of faith," for it "has no dogmatic force." I maintain this still. I say, in spite of Professor Schulte, and the English Catholic writer to whom Mr. Gladstone refers, p. 32, I have as much right to maintain that the implicit condemnation with which it visits its eighty propositions is not *ex cathedra,* or an act of the Infallible Chair, as have those " gravest theologians," as Bishop Fessler speaks, who call its dogmatic force in question, *Fessler,* p. 91. I do not know what Fessler himself says of it more than that it is to be received with submission and obedience. I do not deny another's right to consider it in his private conscience an act of infallibility, or to say, in Mr. Gladstone's words, p. 35, that "utterances *ex cathedra* are not the only form in which Infallibility can speak ;" I only say that I have a right to think otherwise. And when the Pope by a letter approves of one writer who writes one way, and of another who writes in another, he makes neither dogmatic, but both allowable. Mr. Gladstone speaks as if what the Pope says to Fr. Schrader undoes what he says to Bishop Fessler ; why not say that his letter to Fessler neutralizes his letter to Schrader ? I repeat, when I speak of minimizing, I am not turning the profession of it into a dogma; men, if they will, may maximize for me, provided they too keep from dogmatizing. This is my position all through these discussions, and must be kept in mind by any fair reasoner.

I grant the Pope has laid a great stress on the Syllabus; he is said in 1867 to have spoken of it as "a regula docendi;" I cannot tell whether *vivâ voce*, or in writing; any how this did not interfere with Fessler's grave theologians in 1871 considering the Pope did not in it teach dogmatically and infallibly. Moreover, how can a list of proscribed propositions be a "rule," except by turning to the Allocutions, &c., in which they are condemned? and in those Allocutions, when we turn to them, we find in what sense, and with what degree of force severally. In itself the Syllabus can be no more than what the Pope calls it, a syllabus or collection of errors. Led by the references inserted in it to the Allocutions, etc., I have ventured to call it something more, viz., a list or index *raisonné*; an idea not attached to it by me first of all, for Père Daniel, in the October of that very year, 1867, tells us, in the "Etudes Religieuses," "Au Syllabus luimeme il ne faut pas demander que le degré de clarté qui convient à une bonne table des matières," p. 514.

But, whether an index or not, and though it have a substantive character, it is at least clear that the only way in which it can be a "rule of teaching" is by its telling us what to avoid; and this consideration will explain what I mean by receiving it with "obedience," which to some persons is a difficult idea, when contrasted with accepting it with faith. I observe then that obedience is concerned with doing, but faith with affirming. Now, when we are told to avoid certain propositions, we are told primarily and directly not to do something;

whereas, in order to affirm, we must have positive
statements put before us   For instance, it is easy to understand, and in our teaching to avoid the proposition,
"Wealth is the first of goods;" but who shall attempt to
ascertain what the affirmative propositions are, one or
more, which are necessarily involved in the prohibition of
such a proposition, and which must be clearly set down
before we can make an act of faith in them?

However, Mr. Gladstone argues, that, since the Pope's
condemnation of the propositions of the Syllabus has, as I
have allowed, a claim on the obedience of Catholics, that
very fact tells decisively against the unfavorable view the
Pope takes of the same ; he thinks I have here made a fatal
admission.   It is *enough*, he says, that the Syllabus
"unquestionably demands obedience;" that is, enough,
whether the propositions condemned in it deserve condemnation or not.   Here are his very words: "What is *conclusive* . . is this, that the obligation to *obey* it is asserted on
all hands ; . . it is *therefore* absolutely superfluous to follow
Dr. Newman through his references to the Briefs and
Allocutions marginally noted," in order to ascertain their
meaning and drift. . . "I *abide* by my account of the *contents* of the Syllabus." p. 36.   That is, the propositions
may be as false as heathenism, but they have this redeem-
ing virtue, that the Pope denounces them.   His judgment
of them may be as true as Scripture, but it carries this
unpardonable sin with it, that it is given with a purpose,
and not as a mere literary flourish.   Therefore I will not
inquire into the propositions at all ; but my original conclusion shall be dogmatic and irreformable.   Stat pro
ratione voluntas.

Supra, p. 87, I have declined to discuss the difficulties
which Mr. Gladstone raises upon our teaching respecting

the marriage contract (on which I still think him either obscure or incorrect), because they do not fall within the scope to which I professed to confine my remarks ; however, his fresh statements, as they are found, *Vat.* p. 28, lead me to say as follows :

The non-Roman marriages in England, he says, " do not at present fall under the foul epithets of Rome. But why? not because we marry . . under the sanctions of religion, for our marriages are, in the eye of the Pope, purely civil marriages, but only for the technical . . . reason that the disciplinary decrees of Trent are not canonically in force in this country, etc."

Here Mr. Gladstone seems to consider that there are only two ways of marrying according to the Catholic teaching; he omits a third, in which we consider the essence of the sacrament to lie. He speaks of civil marriage, and of marriage " under the sanctions of religion," by which phrase he seems to mean marriage with a rite and a minister. But it is also a *religious* marriage, if the parties, without a priest, by a mutual act of consent, as in the presence of God, marry themselves ; and such a vow of each to other is, according to our theology, really the constituting act, the matter and form, the sacrament of marriage. That is, he omits the very contract which we specially call marriage. This being the case, it follows that every clause of the above passage is incorrect.

1. Mr. Gladstone says, that English non-Roman marriages are held valid at . Rome, *not* because they are contracted " under the sanctions of religion." On the contrary this is the very reason why they are held valid there ; viz., only because parties who have already received the Christian rite of Baptism, proceed to give themselves to each other in the sight of God sacramentally, though they may not call it a sacrament.

L

2. Mr. Gladstone says, "our marriages are in the eye of the Pope *purely civil* marriages." Just the reverse, speaking, as he is, of Church of England marriages. They are considered, in the case of baptized persons, sacramental marriages.

3. Mr. Gladstone says, that they are received at Rome as valid, "*only for the technical,* &c., reason that the disciplinary decrees of Trent are not canonically in force in this country. There is nothing, unless it be motives of mere policy, to prevent the Pope from giving them [those decrees] force here, when he pleases. If, and when that is done, *every marriage thereafter concluded in the English* Church, will, according to his own words, be '*a filthy concubinage.*'" This is not so; I quote to the point two sufficient authorities, St. Alfonso Liguori and Archbishop Kenrick.

Speaking of the clandestinity of marriage (that is, when it is contracted without parish priest and witnesses,) as an impediment to its validity, St. Alfonso says :—" As regards non-Catholics (infideles), or Catholics who live in non-Catholic districts, *or* where the Council of Trent has not been received . . *such a marriage is valid.*" Tom. viii, p. 67, ed. 1845. Even then though the discipline of Trent *was* received in England, still it would not cease to be a Protestant country, and therefore marriages in Protestant churches would be valid.

Archbishop Kenrick is still more explicit. He says :—" Constat Patres Tridentinos legem ita tulisse, ut hæreticorum cætus jam ab Ecclesià divulsos non respiceret . . . . Hoc igitur clandestinitatis impedimentum ad hæreticos seorsim convenientes in locis ubi grassantur hæreses, non est extendendum." Theol. Mor. t. 3, p. 351.

Such being the Catholic rule as to recognition of Protestant marriages, the Pope could not, as Mr. Gladstone thinks, any day invalidate English Protestant marriages by introducing into England the discipline of Trent. The only case, in which any opportunity might occur to the Pope, according to his accusation, of playing fast and loose, is when there was a doubt whether the number of Protestants in a Catholic country was large enough to give them a clear footing there, or when the Government refused to recognize them. Whether such an opportunity has practically occurred and has ever been acted on, I have not the knowledge either to affirm or deny.

§ 8.

Supr. p. 97. "But if the fact be so that the Fathers were not unanimous, is the definition valid ? This depends on the question whether unanimity, at least moral, is or is not necessary for its validity." Vid. also p. 99.

It should be borne in mind that these letters of mine were not intended for publication, and are introduced into my text as documents of 1870, with a view of refuting the false reports of my bearing at that time towards the Vatican Council and Definition. To alter their wording would have been to destroy their argumentative value. I said nothing to imply that on reflection I agreed to every proposition which I set down on my *primâ facie* view of the matter.

One passage of it, perhaps from my own fault, Mr. Gladstone has misunderstood. He quotes me *Vat.* p. 13, as holding that "a definition which the Pope approves, is not absolutely binding thereby, but requires a moral unanimity, and a subsequent reception by the Church." Nay, I considered that the Pope could define without either majority or minority ; but that, if he chose to go by the method of a Council, in that case a moral unanimity was required of its Fathers. I say a few lines lower down, waving the difficulty altogether, " Our merciful Lord would

not care so little for His people . . . as to allow their visible
head and such a large number of Bishops to lead them into
error." Père Ramière, in his very kind review of me in
the *Etudes Religieuses* for February, speaks of the notion
of a moral unanimity as a piece of Gallicanism ; but any
how it has vanished altogether from theology now, since
the Pope, if the Bishops in the Council, few or many, held
back, might define a doctrine without them. A council of
Bishops of the world around him, is only one of the various
modes in which he exercises his infallibility. The seat of
infallibility is in him, and they are adjuncts. The Pastor
Æternus says, "Romani Pontifices, prout temporum et
rerum conditio suadebat, *nunc* convocatis œcumenicis con-
ciliis, *aut* rogatâ Ecclesiæ per orbem dispersæ sententiâ,
nunc per synodos particulares, *nunc* aliis, quæ Divina
suppeditabat Providentia, adhibitis auxiliis, ea tenenda
definiverunt, quæ sacris Scripturis et Apostolicis Tradi-
tionibus consentanea, Deo adjutore, cognoverant."

Nor have I spoken of a subsequent reception by the
Church as entering into the necessary conditions of a *de
fide* decision. I said that by the "Securus judicat orbis
terrarum" all acts of the rulers of the Church are "ratified,"
p. 98. In this passage of my private letter I meant by "ratified" brought home to us as authentic. At this very moment
it is certainly the handy, obvious, and serviceable argument
for our accepting the Vatican definition of the Pope's Infallibility.

Supr. p. 100. I have said that the definition at
Ephesus seemed to be carried by 124 votes against 111 ;
as this was professedly only an inference of my own, I
withdraw it. Confining myself to the facts of the
history, which are perplexed, I observe :—The Council was
opened by St. Cyril on June 22 of the current year,

without waiting for the Bishops representing the great
Syrian patriarchate, who were a few days' journey from
Ephesus, in spite of the protest on that account of 68 of the
Bishops already there. The numbers present at the opening
are given in the Acts as about 150. The first Session, in
which Nestorius was condemned and a definition or exposition of faith made, was concluded before night. That
exposition, as far as the Acts record, was contained in one
of the letters of St. Cyril to Nestorius, which the Bishops
in the Council one by one accepted as conformable to Apostolic teaching. Whether a further letter of St. Cyril's
with his 12 anathematisms, which was also received by the
Bishops, was actually accepted by them as their dogmatic
utterance, is uncertain ; though the Bishops distinctly tell
the Pope and the Emperor that they have accepted it as
well as the others, as being in accordance with the Catholic
Creed. At the end of the acts of the first Session the
signatures of about 200 Bishops are found, and writers of
the day confirm this number, though there is nothing to
show that the additional 40 or 50 were added on the day on
which the definition was passed, June 22, and it is more
probable that they were added afterwards ; *vid.* Tillemont,
Cyril, note 34, and Fleury, *Hist.* xxv. 42. And thus Tillemont, *ibid.*, thinks that the signatures in favour of Cyril
altogether amounted to 220. The Legates of the Pope
were not present ; but they had arrived by July 10. The
Syrian Bishops arrived on June 26th or 27th. As to Africa,
then overrun by the Vandals, it was represented only by
the deacon of the Bishop of Carthage, who sent him to
make his apologies for Africa, to warn the Council against
the Pelagians, and to testify the adherence of the African
Churches to Apostolic doctrine. The countries which were
represented at the Council, and took part in the definition
were Egypt, Asia Minor, and Thrace, Greece, &c. The
whole number of Bishops in Christendom at the time was

about 1,800 ; not 6,000, as St. Dalmatius says at random. Gibbon says, " The Catholic Church was administered by the spiritual and legal jurisdiction of 1,800 bishops, of whom 1,000 were seated in the Greek, and 800 in the Latin provinces of the empire." He adds, " The numbers are not ascertained by any ancient writer or original catalogue ; for the partial lists of the eastern churches are comparatively modern. The patient diligence of Charles à S. Paolo, of Luke Holstein, and of Bingham, has laboriously investigated all the episcopal sees of the Catholic Church."

§ 9.

Supra, pp. 111, etc. It has been objected to the explanation I have given from Fessler and others of the nature and range of the Pope's infallibility as now a dogma of the Church, that it was a lame and impotent conclusion of the Council, if so much effort was employed, as is involved in the convocation and sitting of an Ecumenical Council, in order to do so little. True, if it were called to do what it did and no more; but that such was its aim is a mere assumption. In the first place it can hardly be doubted that there were those in the Council who were desirous of a stronger definition ; and the definition actually made, as being moderate, is so far the victory of those many bishops who considered any definition on the subject inopportune. And it was no slight fruit of the proceedings in the Council, if a definition was to be, to have effected a moderate definition. But the true answer to the objection is that which is given by Bishop Ullathorne. The question of the Pope's infallibility was not one of the objects professed in convening the Council; and the Council is not yet ended.

He says in his "Expostulation Unravelled," "The expostulation goes on to suggest that the council was cno-

vened mainly with a view of defining the infallibility, and
that the definition itself was brought about, chiefly for
political objects, through the action of the Pontiff and a
dominant party. A falser notion could not be entertained. I have the official catalogue before me of the
Schemata prepared by the theologians for discussion in
the council. In them the infallibility is not even mentioned; for the greater part of them regard ecclesiastical
discipline." P. 48, he adds, "Calamitous events suspended
the Council."

Supr. p. 116, note. I have referred to Bishop Fessler's
statement that only the last sentences of Boniface's *Unam
Sanctam* are infallible. To this Mr. Gladstone replies
p. 45, that the word " Porro," introducing the final words
to which the anathema is affixed, extends that anathema
to the body of the Bull, which precedes the " Porro." But
he does not seem to have observed that there are two
distinct heresies condemned in the Bull, and that the
" Porro" is the connecting link between these two condemnations, that is, between the penultima and final sentences.
The Pope first says " Nisi duo, sicut Manichæus, fingat esse
principia, *quod falsum et hæreticum judicamus* . . . porro,
subesse Romano Pontifici, omni humanæ creaturæ declaramus, definimus, et pronunciamus omnino esse de necessi-
tate salutis." That the Latin is deficient in classical
terseness and perspicuity we may freely grant.

Supra, p. 117, I say, "We call 'infallibility' in the case
of the apostles, inspiration; in the case of the church,
assistentia."

On this Mr. Gladstone says, "On such a statement I
have two remarks to make; first, we have this assurance
on the strength only of *his own private judgment*, p. 102."
How can he say so when, p. 132, I quote Father Perrone,

saying, " *Never have Catholics* taught that the gift of in-
fallibillity is given by God to the Church after the manner
of inspiration!"

Mr. Gladstone proceeds, " Secondly, that, if bidden
by the self-assertion of the Pope, he will be required by
his principles to retract it,and to assert, if occasion should
arise, the contrary." I can only say to so hypothetical an
argument what is laid down by Fessler and the Swiss
bishops, that the Pope cannot, by virtue of his infallibility,
reverse what has always been held ; and that the "inspiration" of the church, in the sense in which the Apostles
were inspired, is contrary to our received teaching. If
Protestants are to speculate about our future, they should
be impartial enough to recollect, that if, on the one hand,
we believe that a Pope can add to our articles of faith, so
on the other, we hold also that a heretical Pope, *ipso facto*,
ceases to be Pope by reason of his heresy.

Mr. Gladstone thus ends : " Thirdly, that he lives
under a system of development, through which somebody's
private opinion of to-day may become matter of faith for
all the to-morrows of the future." I think he should give
some proof of this ; let us have one instance in which
" somebody's private opinion" has become *de fide*. Instead
of this he geos on to assert (interrogatively) that Popes, *e.g.*
Clement XI. and Gregory II., and the present Pope, have
claimed the inspiration of the Apostles, and that Germans,
Italians, French, have ascribed such a gift to him;—of
course he means theologians, not mere courtiers or syco-
phants, for the Pope cannot help having such, till human
nature is changed. If Mr. Gladstone is merely ha-
ranguing as an Orator, I do not for an instant quarrel
with him or attempt to encounter him ; but, if he is a
controversialist, we have a right to look for arguments, not
mere assertions.